PERSONALIZED READING

Digital Strategies and Tools to Support All Learners

INTERNATIONAL SOCIETY FOR TECHNOLOGY IN EDUCATION
PORTLAND, OR · ARLINGTON, VA

MICHELE HAIKEN WITH L. ROBERT FURMAN

DEDICATION
For Max and Sadie

PERSONALIZED READING
Digital Strategies and Tools to Support All Learners
Michele Haiken with L. Robert Furman

ACQUISITIONS EDITOR: Valerie Witte
DEVELOPMENT AND COPY EDITOR: Linda Laflamme
PROOFREADER: Corinne Gould
INDEXER: Wendy Allex
BOOK DESIGN AND PRODUCTION: Danielle Foster
COVER DESIGN: Eddie Ouellette

LIBRARY OF CONGRESS CATALOGING-IN-PUBLICATION DATA AVAILABLE

FIRST EDITION
ISBN: 978-1-56484-687-7
Ebook version available
Printed in the United States of America
ISTE® is a registered trademark of the International Society for Technology in Education.

ABOUT ISTE

The International Society for Technology in Education (ISTE) is the premier nonprofit organization serving educators and education leaders committed to empowering connected learners in a connected world. ISTE serves more than 100,000 education stakeholders throughout the world.

ISTE's innovative offerings include the ISTE Conference & Expo, one of the biggest, most comprehensive ed tech events in the world—as well as the widely adopted ISTE Standards for learning, teaching, and leading in the digital age and a robust suite of professional learning resources, including webinars, online courses, consulting services for schools and districts, books, and peer-reviewed journals and publications. Visit iste.org to learn more.

JOIN OUR COMMUNITY OF PASSIONATE EDUCATORS

ISTE members get free year-round professional development opportunities and discounts on ISTE resources and conference registration. Membership also connects you to a network of educators who can instantly help with advice and best practices.

Join or renew your ISTE membership today!

Visit iste.org/membership or call 800.336.5191.

RELATED ISTE TITLES

Gamify Literacy: Boost Comprehension, Collaboration and Learning, edited by Michele Haiken

Teaching Literacy in the Digital Age: Inspiration for All Levels and Literacies, edited by Mark Gura

Technology, Reading & Digital Literacy: Strategies to Engage the Reluctant Reader, by L. Robert Furman

To see all books available from ISTE, please visit iste.org/resources.

ABOUT THE AUTHORS

MICHELE HAIKEN, ED.D. has been teaching literacy for twenty years. A lifelong learner, Haiken is a middle school English teacher and an adjunct professor of literacy at Manhattanville College in Purchase, NY. She is the editor of the book *Gamify Literacy* and author of the blog *The Teaching Factor* (theteachingfactor.com), where she shares ideas for digital technology and literacy in the classroom to bolster student success. A member of ISTE's Literacy PLN, she moderates #ISTELitChat, a monthly Twitter chat discussing digital literacy. Throughout the U.S., Haiken has spoken on the subjects of literacy, technology, and gamification. She lives in Stamford, CT, with her family. You can connect with her on Twitter @teachingfactor.

L. ROBERT FURMAN, ED.D., is an educator, leader, and speaker, as well as the author of *The Future-Ready Challenge* and *Technology, Reading & Digital Literacy*. He has received numerous awards, including being named one of the National School Board Association's 2015 "20 to Watch" in technology education. He is a podcast host and founding member of the Council on the Future of Education, and he is the principal at South Park Elementary Center near Pittsburgh, Pennsylvania.

ACKNOWLEDGMENTS

This book is an evolution of my experiences teaching and learning. The authors and educators referenced throughout this book have been my teachers and mentors. They have left an imprint on my teaching and educational philosophies and have made me the educator I am today. Additionally, my own professional learning network, which has expanded exponentially through ISTE and on Twitter, has made me a better teacher today and every day. The global connections made through social media are instrumental.

I am grateful to my principal at Rye Middle School, Dr. Ann Edwards, who has always been supportive of my teaching and piloting new technology. I am so lucky to work in a school district with many amazing teachers, particularly my colleagues Peter Gouveia, Francesca Miller, and Marissa Curcio. Your expertise and passion for teaching and learning are infectious, and I am grateful for your friendship, collaboration, and support.

My students both in middle school and on the graduate level inspire me every day and push me to think of new and engaging ways to teach English and support their literacy learning. Your questions and curiosity fuel my love of teaching.

To my editor, Valerie Witte, at ISTE, thank you for always listening, reading, and supporting my ideas. Both Valerie and Emily Reed have been great to work with and have helped bring this book to fruition. Linda Laflamme, you are a word wizard, and your insight and suggestions helped to articulate the ideas presented in this book with clarity and precision.

Thank you to my family; without them I would not have gotten this far. My mother and sister, in particular, encouraged me to share my ideas and publish. To my husband and children who are always there for me and by my side, thank you for your unconditional support even when you were nudging me to get off the computer. Now you have my undivided attention. Remember, the world is your text. Continue to read it critically, closely, and with compassion. Never stop learning.

CONTENTS

CHAPTER 3 # ENGLISH LANGUAGE LEARNERS . . . 42

CHAPTER 4 # ADVANCED READERS 64

FOREWORD

Our reading lives are evolving, growing in ways that are both exhilarating and overwhelming. As educators we interact with text inside and outside the classroom, navigating across blog posts, social media streams, newspaper articles, and book club novels. The reading experiences we have begun to embrace mirror the behaviors we want our students to explore, practice and master as readers.

All learners can benefit from practicing strategies to help us find the balance between the power of print and digital reading materials.

If you walk into a tech-rich classroom of readers, you will find students navigating a new world of literature and informational text. In a classroom of readers, you might find a small group of students discussing a current events article in one corner, or a student deep into a story at a desk or beanbag chair diving into a book on their own. Digital tools empower educators to support their students and give children of all ages an opportunity to develop their own reading lives—tailored to their needs, passions, and goals for lifelong learning.

I first met Michele Haiken at an edcamp in Manhattanville College where her passion for professional learning and community building produced an event that drew educators from across the region and beyond. Michele's enthusiasm for literacy instruction and her knowledge of the research and reasoning behind technology integration shines throughout this book.

As educators introduce a range of technology into classroom environments, there is a sense of opportunity we simply have not seen before. Transformations are taking place with the way all readers interact with text, respond to reading, apply new information, and share their learning.

All readers in today's classroom benefit from the strategic, purposeful integration of digital tools. When chosen thoughtfully, with clear connections to learning goals, they can help transform traditional reading experiences to address the needs of all readers with diverse needs, interests, and experiences. I often use the phrase *tasks before apps* to describe the idea of putting the learning first in tech-rich classrooms. *Personalized Reading: Digital Strategies and Tools to Support All Learners* examines the different readers present in today's classrooms and identifies their needs. Technology doesn't have to be bright, shiny, or flashy to elevate teaching and learning. It must be used purposefully and strategically—a concept embraced in the pages you are about to explore.

It is essential that classrooms in all corners of the world leverage digital tools to prepare students for reading in every sense of the word. Navigating a world of digital text in short, long, and mixed-media forms is just the tip of the iceberg. Students in today's classrooms will be asked to read, respond, and share in online spaces and virtual places, and in all the ways we've loved sharing our reading lives in classrooms of the past.

Preparing students for college, careers, and lifelong reading experiences must include the integration of digital tools. Our students already interact with content and media that mirror experiences of professionals across industries. Children of all ages can search on a smartphone for a video to help them answer a question, click on a hyperlink as they read on a tablet, or take notes on their laptop as they research a topic. This puts educators in an exciting and important position to take advantage of the ways digital tools provide relevancy and context for reading across and beyond the school day.

Now more than ever, educators, families, and readers of all ages have a clear call to action. What are we doing today, tomorrow, and in the weeks ahead to prepare students for an ever-evolving world? Michele Haiken and L. Robert Furman present a compelling case and clear action steps for educators who are ready to move the needle, light a fire, and prepare readers for a digital world!

—Monica Burns, Ed.D., author of *Tasks Before Apps: Designing Rigorous Learning in a Tech-Rich Classroom* and *#FormativeTech: Meaningful, Sustainable, and Scalable Formative Assessment with Technology*

INTRODUCTION

To be successful learners, students need to be proficient readers. In fact, the higher the grade level, the more often students are expected to learn content-specific information and master the curriculum through reading—chapters in science and history textbooks, nonfiction articles, primary documents, literature, and more. By the time students enter middle school and high school, the assumption is that they *all* know how to read well—but they don't. At a point in their school careers when they are required to read dense text to extract content information, many students still struggle to comprehend the assigned texts. Their reading proficiency may even be below grade level.

Contrary to the traditional assumption, classrooms serve a broad spectrum of readers: some are struggling, some reluctant, others advanced, and still others are English language learners (ELL). Within these four broad categories, you may find students who read only to look for answers, who are skimmers and glossers, who look for an escape in reading, or who are readers looking for help. You might even have other types of readers in your class beyond these. Teaching reading can no longer be "one size fits all." We need a variety of approaches—and for a variety of mediums. Teachers must not only addresses functional literacy that includes reading of visual, print, and digital text, but that also encourages students to be critical consumers of information in order to effectively communicate their thinking about these texts.

Nor is reading a one-and-done skill picked up in elementary school that can automatically be used successfully in higher grades. Reading is a lifelong skill that must be continually honed. For this reason, teachers today are called upon not only to teach their content areas, but to teach readers as well. Educators and authors Harvey Daniels and Nancy Steineke (2011) stated, "We are all expected to be reading teachers." Teaching reading does not, and should not, end with elementary school. No matter the grade level, all teachers need to support a range of readers, meeting students where they are at in their reading proficiency.

How, you may ask, can you meet the needs of *all* the learners so they become deep readers who think critically and communicate effectively about the information they interact with? That's the central question this book aims to answer, but there is no single quick fix. Teaching the *reader* not the text, offering book choice, establishing reading workshops, utilizing print and visual texts, and making the best use of technology are approaches that dominate the discussion on teaching reading today.

Technology, especially, has allowed teachers to diversify their teaching even more and provides leverage for all students to succeed. More important than the technology tools you use, however, is that you create meaningful classroom experiences with them to promote reading, critical thinking, and digital literacy. As Harvard professor and author Christopher Dede said, "Technology is not fire. You cannot stand next to it and expect to reap the benefits. Technology is more like clothes, you have to put it on to figure it out and get it to fit right" (2017). But, with so many amazing technology apps, platforms, and tools being released every day, how do you find that right fit? This book can help.

Personalized Reading: Digital Strategies and Tools to Support All Learners grew from Rob Furman's *Technology, Reading & Digital Literacy: Strategies to Engage the Reluctant Reader* (2015), which highlighted technology tools to help reluctant readers find, discuss, and share books. Rob and I sat down together to elaborate and expand on his book to address engaging *all* readers with additional teaching ideas, strategies, and resources. We realized this was a completely different book adding depth in the technology choices and teaching techniques highlighted. Although we collaborated early on in the project, the teaching ideas presented throughout the book are based on my experiences. The more I brainstormed and talked through ideas with Rob, however, the more I realized that before I could write about tools and teaching techniques I needed to define the habits of proficient readers.

STRATEGIES OF PROFICIENT READERS

Pearson and Dole's (1991) research on reading determined that proficient readers, or "good readers," employ a number of comprehension strategies before, during, and after reading. These comprehension skills include:

Before Reading

✦ Survey the reading and assignment.

✦ Activate background knowledge.

✦ Understand the task.

During Reading

✦ Read actively: Highlight or underline important facts and information.

✦ Code or write important notes in the margins or use sticky notes to record ideas, questions, predictions, and responses.

✦ Make connections with what I already know or have experienced.

✦ Monitor comprehension.

✦ Visualize to enhance comprehension.

✦ Make inferences, conclusions, evaluations, and interpretations.

After Reading

✦ Reflect: What did I learn? How is this important?

✦ Summarize.

✦ Synthesize and extend my thinking.

Proficient readers make predictions, notice patterns, and infer. When they finish reading the text, they are able to summarize, evaluate, and analyze it. As Harvey and Goudvis (2007) reported, proficient readers "have an inner conversation with the writer and the text. It's as if they are talking to the text while reading" (p. 4). The reader might "talk back to text" by asking questions, making predictions, connecting their own experiences, and even debating with the author. Proficient readers have habits of thinking that help them to make meaning and understand the text more deeply.

Proficient readers are capable of utilizing many skills when they are reading to help them comprehend and understand the text. Additionally, they are aware of which skills to use when they read for content in school or when reading a challenging text. For example, they may annotate the text to highlight the important details or annotate their thinking while reading, asking questions and making predictions in the margins or on sticky notes. Some of these skills happen automatically, such as visualizing or making predictions, whereas other skills are put into practice to monitor comprehension only after the reader decides what is important, such as rereading the text when a reader realizes at the end of the page they do not know what the passage was about. A proficient reader is able to retell and summarize the events in the text. They might also make connections while they are reading, associating the events in the text with other texts or personal experience.

Think about yourself as a reader for a moment. What reading and thinking strategies do you employ when reading for information or to build understanding? Read through the Reading Strategies Assessment in Table I.1, and check the appropriate column to indicate whether or not you use each strategy. Identifying your own strategies will help you uncover your own reading processes, which might have been invisible beforehand. When we "think about our thinking," we are applying metacognition. This thinking and knowing helps readers comprehend texts and monitor their reading. Gravity Goldberg (2016) called on teachers to be "mentors, models, and guides by demonstrating, naming and modeling" (p. 136) the habits of proficient readers and to support students throughout the reading process. Once we recognize our own reading strategies, we can mentor the readers in our own classroom.

TABLE I.1 READING STRATEGY ASSESSMENT

READING STRATEGY ASSESSMENT	YES	NO
Activate schema or background knowledge. Ask yourself, *What do I already know about this topic?*		
Ask questions while reading to clarify and deepen understanding. Ask yourself, *What does the author want me to know?*		
Infer by using background knowledge and clues from the text to draw conclusions about the text. Ask yourself, *What information do I need to make sense of this topic?*		
Determine importance. Ask yourself, *What is the main idea?*		
Monitor comprehension and use appropriate strategies when confused. Ask yourself, *Does this make sense? If I reread will it help me gain a better understanding?*		
Visualize the reading. Ask yourself, *Does a movie play in my mind's eye that helps me understand the text?*		
Synthesize and extend your thinking. Ask yourself, *What did I learn from the reading, and how does it grow or change my thinking?*		

How did you do? Most readers use a few of these strategies, but there's no magic number that's correct or optimal. Now, think about the students in your classroom. Whether in elementary school, middle school, or high school, students are still building their reading abilities. Even proficient or advanced readers may be using only *some* of these strategies, but not all. Readers who struggle may not use any effectively.

Just like adding technology for the sake of using it, teaching students reading strategies in isolation is not the answer. Cris Tovani stated, "teaching strategies for the sake of teaching strategies isn't the goal. Being able to make connections or ask questions or visualize isn't what matters most. The only reason to teach kids how to be strategic readers is to help them become more thoughtful about their reading" (2004, p. 9). All readers need strategy *practice*, rather than strategies in isolation. Research shows when students are using several reading strategies, they are able to handle texts at or above grade level. Thus, teachers need to be more thoughtful with the texts, techniques, and tools they use with students.

HOW THIS BOOK CAN HELP

What can content area teachers do to increase proficiency? I'm not suggesting you interrupt your Earth science or global history curriculum to offer a reading lesson once a week (although it doesn't hurt to read aloud in class and model your own thinking while reading for students). I know from my own classroom experiences that teaching strategies in isolation takes away from the heart of reading. While we all want our students to be proficient readers and critical thinkers, we also want them to enjoy reading and find pleasure in a great book. One of the goals of *Personalized Reading* is to inspire you to think beyond the text and help students not only learn how to read, but also how to read to learn, thus increasing their knowledge and coming full circle.

Throughout this book, you will learn how to approach the spectrum of readers in your classroom to empower them each with skills and strategies for success. With a distillation of my teaching experience, conversations with Rob, and extensive research, each chapter addresses meaningful approaches for teaching readers and suggests classroom-proven technology tools that will help students become creative communicators, knowledge constructors, empowered learners, and responsible contributors to the digital world. In today's digital culture, teachers are asking students to be critical consumers of *all* texts: audio, visual, and printed. *Personalized Reading*, therefore, addresses using reading strategies with all types of text from traditional print to movies and animated shorts to podcasts and digital texts.

As in Rob's *Technology, Reading & Digital Literacy*, the tools and techniques I share in this book are to match students with the books and digital content that inspire them to read, question, and connect, empowering them as learners. All teaching techniques can be adapted for diverse content areas, multiple grade levels, and the needs of your class. Remember, there is no one way to do this.

The first four chapters in this book each highlight specific readers—struggling readers, reluctant readers, English language learners, and advanced readers—while the final chapter offers strategies for teaching the mix of proficiencies found in all of our classrooms:

+ **CHAPTER 1** identifies *struggling readers* and how digital reading platforms can help to support them with the necessary scaffolding and skill practice to improve comprehension. From podcasts to blogs and beyond, this chapter also will show you where to look for new book recommendations to offer "just right" choices for students to read and discuss.

+ **CHAPTER 2** addresses *reluctant readers*. It focuses on using visual text as a bridge to practice close reading strategies and help students read images and film critically, as they would printed text. You'll also find suggestions on pairing books and films, as well as storyboarding activities to encourage student understanding.

✦ **CHAPTER 3** looks closely at the digital tools to help *English language learners* build background knowledge and vocabulary, as well as speaking activities to build communication skills. This chapter spotlights virtual reality (VR) and augmented reality (AR) field trips as tools to immerse students in learning.

✦ **CHAPTER 4** seeks to provide *advanced readers* with their own strategies and technology tools that foster independence and higher-level thinking skills. This chapter explains how to use Twitter as a tool for student-led book discussions with their class- and schoolmates, interacting with authors, and sharing the love of reading.

✦ **CHAPTER 5** centers on *teaching diverse readers together* because classrooms are heterogeneous places. This chapter presents a collection of ideas for making your classroom a dynamic, empowering atmosphere for learning at all levels. You'll investigate flipped learning, differentiated choices, global collaborative projects, Genius Hour and Passion Projects, and adventure-based learning opportunities for students to work at their own pace to meet learning targets.

Each chapter introduces a variety of technology tools, teaching techniques, and classroom examples. QR codes placed throughout the book will help you connect with key technology tools, books, and media. At the end of each chapter, recommended techniques and tools are paired with the Common Core State Standards, ISTE Standards for Students, and ISTE Standards for Educators (International Society for Technology in Education [ISTE], 2016 and 2017) that they support in an easy-to-reference table titled "Pairing Tools with Teaching Strategies." These same tables also provide the links you'll need to find out more about all the chapter's recommended resources.

AS YOU GO FORWARD

The readers in our classrooms are individuals with unique needs and preferences. Technology allows us to offer learning experiences to support these diverse student learners. As Alabama principal Danny Steele stated on Twitter, "It is good to know content. It is great to know pedagogy. It's imperative to know the kids" (2018). Once teachers get to know their kids, they can incorporate meaningful and thoughtful learning experiences for all their learners. This book is intended to help you access the tools and techniques to help your students to read, think critically, and discover meaning in the text they read.

CHAPTER 1

STRUGGLING READERS

Everyone is smart in different ways.

But if you judge a fish on its ability to climb a tree,

it will spend its whole life thinking that it's stupid.

—Lynda Mullaly Hunt, *Fish in a Tree*; and Albert Einstein

Struggling readers read below grade level and are behind their peers. Whether a learning disability or, as Karen Tankersley (2005) put it, their "own lack of skill" (p. 3) is at the heart of the issue, they might struggle with decoding, comprehension, or both. Identifying struggling readers is the first step in supporting them and building their reading proficiency. Beginning with reading assessments can help you identify the strengths and weaknesses of your readers, plus the data you collect will help you bring in more effective supports for your students so they can build the skills of a proficient reader.

This chapter presents various supports and technology tools you can use with struggling readers—from digital reading platforms to audiobooks and podcasts to metacognition strategies. As you'll learn, reading platforms provide a variety of texts, leveled reading, and customization for you to help struggling readers make progress in understanding deeply, making connections, and thinking critically for personal insight and reflection. Because listening is one of the Common Core State Standards' Anchor Standards (CCSS.ELA-Literacy.CCRA.SL.2), building reading skills with audio books, read-alouds, and podcasts addresses multiple learning needs at once. Along the way, you'll also learn about some sources to tap when hunting for new titles to pique the interest of not only struggling readers, but perhaps their classmates too.

BUILDING A POSITIVE EXPERIENCE WITH READING

One thing that is particularly important when working with struggling readers is to keep the reading experience positive. If a student is having difficulty reading, you must provide the student with positive experiences that will make him or her want to continue reading. Additionally, helping struggling readers to get the right books and texts in their hands is vital. For example, books that are too challenging will frustrate struggling readers. When students try to read at their frustration level, they quickly lose incentive to read and become reluctant readers; it's a perfect storm that creates haters of reading. In other words, if you make a student read a challenging text without supports or opportunities for success, that student might go on to become a reluctant reader. Likewise, you don't want students reading at a lower level than they're capable of, because they will become bored and complacent. Bored students are at equal risk to become reluctant readers. Finding the "just right book" for each and every student in the classroom is a quest for all teachers, and the two most common guides to follow are reading levels and student choice.

READING LEVELS AS A GUIDE TO SUPPORT STRUGGLING READERS

Richard Allington (2013) stated, "What benefits children who struggle with learning to read the most is a steady diet of high-quality reading lessons, lessons in which they have texts they can read with an appropriate level of accuracy and in which they are also engaged in the sort of work we expect our better readers to do" (p. 527). To find those appropriate texts, many elementary school teachers use Lexile scores or scores from a DRA (Developmental Reading Assessment) or DIBELS (Dynamic Indicators of Basic Early Literacy Skills) assessment to help evaluate students' reading comprehension and reading capabilities. You can use a standard reading assessment or create your own reading inventory. Either way, the scores can help you pinpoint reading instruction, as well as match readers with books of interest that are on their reading levels.

Even when you have an idea of a student's reading level, where can you find content at that level that will engage the student? Struggling readers need "accessible text—text that is interesting, well written, and appropriately matched to the level of the students" (Tovani, 2000, p. 39), and you can find it online. For example, the reading platforms Newsela and Actively Learn, as well as the Wonderopolis website offer accessible text that you can use to build comprehension and conversations in the classroom. The following sections examine each option more closely.

NEWSELA

Specializing in nonfiction articles, the Newsela instructional content and reading platform offers articles on a vast array of subjects (current events, history, science, literature, and more) and at multiple Lexile reading levels. Newsela enables you to search thousands of articles and text sets, which are collections of articles on a common topic, theme, or reading standard (**FIGURE 1.1**). To make it easier for you to share the same article with the variety of learners in your classroom, Newsela adapts its articles to several Lexile levels, so you can assign the same article to your whole class and still offer personalized reading. No matter what their reading proficiency, students can all work on the same article and be contributing members of the classroom, but each can work at his or her prescribed level without being frustrated or bored.

FIGURE 1.1
The Newsela reading platform organizes its articles by topic and offers versions of the same article in multiple Lexile levels.

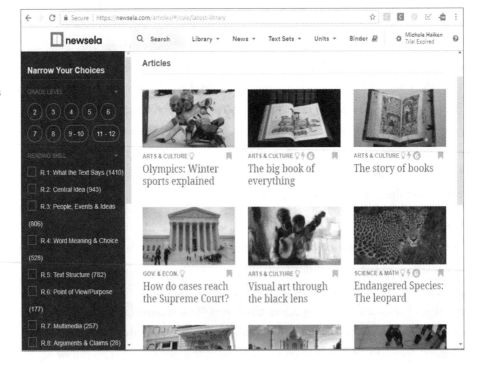

Newsela is available free for teachers and students, or you can upgrade to the subscription-based PRO version. In both versions, Newsela embeds quizzes, annotations, and writing prompts with every reading. The PRO edition adds such features as the ability to view individual student progress, to track student progress against the Common Core State Standards, and for students and teachers to see each other's article annotations.

Similar to Malcolm Gladwell's 10,000 hours concept in his book *Outliers* (2008), research shows that the more students read, the more their reading fluency and comprehension improves (Guthrie, Schafer, & Von Secker, 2000). Whether you offer digital texts through Newsela's online platform or have students read paper copies of the texts, the more students read, the more their reading and comprehension improves.

ACTIVELY LEARN

Similar to Newsela, Actively Learn offers a catalog of articles and texts suitable for elementary and secondary students, although it does not differentiate by Lexile levels. You can assign texts for your students to read, as well as embed questions, polls, and writing assessments throughout the reading. You can also embed media and hyperlinks in the text to help guide student reading and thinking. Another benefit to Actively Learn is that it offers not only pre-made reading lessons with questions aligned to cited Common Core State Standards, but also the ability for you to upload your own text. To create customized reading assignments for your students, you can then add multiple-choice or short-answer reading response questions to your text.

While reading their assigned text online on Actively Learn, students can highlight key ideas and mark confusing passages by flagging a section or asking a question. Teachers can see these questions and respond by inserting private, in-text guidance—no need to single out and possibly embarrass struggling readers by necessitating them to ask in front of the whole class. In turn, you can use the data collected through the student responses, flags, and questions to better tailor instruction. If a student doesn't know the meaning of a word, right-clicking on the word brings up a menu, from which the student can choose to see a definition, translate the word, or hear the word read aloud. If you post reading-response questions at key points throughout the reading, students cannot read beyond a question until they answer it. Additionally, Actively Learn lets students translate the text in different languages or hear the text read aloud, enabling ELL students to read in their home language and struggling students to comprehend the text.

Customizing assignments with a digital platform, such as Actively Learn, leads to more effective and independent instruction that targets students' strengths and weaknesses by giving support to students that need it, while omitting it for those who don't. For example, I use Actively Learn with my eighth-grade students weekly. Borrowing from Kelly Gallagher's "Article of the Week" assignment (2004), I assign students an article on Actively Learn to read at the beginning of the week and then ask them to write an extended response about their reading and thinking about the text. With my students' abilities and strengths in mind, I select articles that complement the current unit of study to build background knowledge and draw connections between texts and current events. For example, when students are reading Harper Lee's *To Kill A Mockingbird* (1960), I assign historical documents to help build students' understanding about the setting and socioeconomic climate in America during the 1930s: FDR's speech "The Only Thing to Fear Is Fear Itself," excerpts from The Scottsboro Boys Trial, an interview with women who grew up in the south during the 1930s that addresses gender codes of the era, poems with thematic connections like "Papa's Waltz" by Theodore Roethke (1942), and biographical information about Harper Lee. When you embed sidebars with additional content and links directly into the text to support and extend information, students feel more active engagement with the text. (See the sidebar, "Getting the Most from a Reading Platform" for other ideas for using Actively Learn.)

Actively Learn is completely customizable in both its paid and free versions. With the free version, you may import as many as three outside articles or documents a month. **FIGURE 1.2** shows my work space on Actively Learn, which lists the most recent titles I've uploaded for classroom use. In exchange for paying a yearly licensing fee, you can upload an unlimited number of texts, plus gain access to more digital texts from classics to contemporary young adult titles.

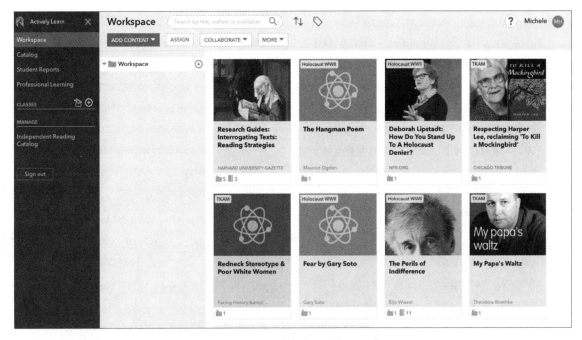

FIGURE 1.2 In the Actively Learn work space, you can label texts by unit for easy accessibility, as well as indicate which texts are assigned or to be assigned to students.

WONDEROPOLIS

For smaller doses of text and nonfiction reading, Wonderopolis offers a daily Wonder, or question, that it then answers with an article and a video for students to read and watch. Whether they want to know what marshmallows are made of or what dark matter is, the free Wonderopolis website enables students to search their own curiosities and explore answers to burning questions. This is a great website for struggling readers because the topics are meant to engage their curiosity. Unlike Newsela and Actively Learn, which enable you to select and assign texts to students, Wonderopolis offers one

GETTING THE MOST FROM A READING PLATFORM

You can use Actively Learn, Newsela, and other reading platforms in a variety of ways to support struggling readers and build content knowledge. For instance, try these activities:

- **JIGSAW.** Using the text sets in Newsela and Actively Learn, you can assign each student a specific text in the set (a single puzzle piece) to read and share with a small group. When the students come together in the small groups, they work collaboratively to find common themes and connections among all the readings and thereby put together the entire jigsaw. (For more ideas for jigsaw activities, see Chapter 4.)

- **CHOICE READING.** In the paid version of Actively Learn, books are available for purchase. Students can choose a particular book they are interested in reading. You can also select and assign multiple readings on a similar topic or theme, and then students can select which of the articles from the controlled choice to read. These choice readings can be used during independent reading or for a specific assignment.

- **BUILDING BACKGROUND KNOWLEDGE.** Actively Learn allows you to embed videos, links, and annotations within a text to help students build background knowledge and further understanding. For example, if students are reading Richard Conniff's article, "When Continental Drift Was Considered Pseudoscience" (*Smithsonian Magazine*, 2012), a National Geographic video of continental drift or HHMI BioInteractive's *Animated Life: Pangea, Wegener, and Continental Drift* (2015) can be embedded into the reading to help students visualize this science concept.

- **DO NOWS AND BELL RINGERS.** When they first arrive, students can begin class with a short reading of a poem or article on Newsela or Actively Learn and answer questions based on the reading. Additionally, you can begin the day with "The Wonder of the Day" on Wonderopolis and have students complete one of the extension activities to show understanding.

- **FLIPPED LEARNING.** You can assign readings, images, and videos on Newsela or Actively Learn for students to read before class. When students enter class, they are ready to participate in an activity, such as a debate or lab experiment, using the information presented in the texts. (For more flipped learning ideas, see Chapter 5.)

text in answer to each Wonder question followed by a list of extension activities to try out. For example, Wonder #2065 describes how a fire extinguisher works and suggests three activities: making a family fire safety plan, taking a field trip to a store to investigate fire extinguishers, and reading a linked article about different types of fire extinguishers. You can choose a Wonder every day to share with your class or allow students to select their own Wonders and explore the website. When students have opportunities to choose texts that they are interested in reading and that are at an appropriate reading level, they will be more receptive to instruction in the skills that will help them become proficient readers.

CAPTURE THEIR INTEREST: OFFERING BOOK CHOICE

Reading scores from standardized tests can be useful tools to find reading material for students, but they should not be the *only* criteria you use. Student interests and needs are equally important to consider. Many struggling readers are able to make sense of books and texts that are beyond their assigned Lexile levels because they are interested, curious, and passionate about the subject. Thus, student choice is essential with young readers to maintain their interest to continue reading and improve their reading abilities. Many of today's leading voices in the classroom and reading educators are in favor of book choice; Robb (2000), Calkins (2001), Kittle (2013), and Miller (2014) encourage choice so students can read books that spark their own passions. Kyleene Beers (2017) reminds us, "Choice never begins with Lexile levels." Instead, as Donalyn Miller (2009) stated, "We must ensure children have meaningful book access all year long. And a thoughtful selection of books in a diversity of formats, levels, and genres." Allowing students to choose their own books is an important step in engaging their interest. Once you have that interest, you can share classroom conversations about what is hard and easy about reading, all the while opening doors to lessons on reading strategies that help students master difficult text and build endurance for more challenges.

Finding meaningful texts and titles to inspire and encourage struggling readers to continue reading can be its own challenge, but a variety of sources can help you learn about noteworthy books to diversify your classroom library. From blogs to podcasts to Twitter chats to chatting with peers at conferences, sharing book recommendations can help you find the right titles to inspire and encourage struggling readers to continue reading.

BLOGS, REVIEWS, AND SOCIAL MEDIA

The Nerdy Book Club is a daily blog on young adult and children's books. Founded by teachers Donalyn Miller and Colby Sharp and written by teachers, writers, and authors, The Nerdy Book Club not only offers reviews and suggestions of thousands of titles across grade levels and themes, but also posts on supporting readers and good reading practices.

Another excellent source for book reviews of any type—from picture books to contemporary titles and classical texts—is Goodreads. Goodreads is a vast website, but you can search for books by genre, subject, and author. The annual Goodreads Choice Awards also highlight noteworthy books.

For more specific book recommendations, social media is a great tool to find book titles and texts specific to subject and genre, award winners, and noteworthy reads to share with students and use in the classroom. Whether searching on Pinterest, following publishers' Facebook pages and Twitter feeds, or consulting library blogs, you'll find book titles are being shared through all mediums.

PODCASTS

For recommendations of books as well as insights about their authors, tune in to *The Yarn*, a free podcast available on iTunes and hosted by librarian Travis Jonker and teacher Colby Sharp. *The Yarn* shares interviews with young adult and children's authors. You can find out about new books on the podcast, as well as learn about the authors themselves. Oftentimes when our students and we learn more about authors and their inspiration for writing, we are drawn into their text. For example, in Episode 56, Angie Thomas talked about the extensive research she did for her book, *The Hate U Give* (2017) and how she used her own emotional response to the Black Lives Matter movement to fuel the emotions of her main character, Star. Listening to the podcast, I also learned that Thomas' "intention in writing the novel was to show hope, community, and love during a time of tremendous frustration and anger" (2017). Thomas' writing draws even struggling readers in quickly, and the book is now in my classroom library.

TWITTER CHATS

Participating in a book club is another great way to learn about new titles suitable for your classroom library, to share your recommendations with peers, and maybe even to read outside your own comfort zone. If organizing or joining a local book club isn't an option, consider joining one online. Twitter, the microblogging social network, provides a network of teachers 24-7 collaboration, connection, and professional development. Specific chats provide opportunities for teachers to interact with others and discuss specific topics. There are Twitter chats by grade levels, content areas, location, and teaching techniques. For a current calendar of Twitter chats by day, time, and topic, check out Education Chats, a Google site maintained by five educators.

In addition, #TitleTalk and #2JennsBookClub are two monthly Twitter chats that discuss recently published young adult and children's books. Started by librarians Jennifer Northrup and Jennifer LaGarde and already in its fifth season, #2JennsBookClub brings together English teachers and librarians to discuss newly released young adult titles once a month on Thursday evenings at 8 p.m. ET. During the last fifteen minutes of many of the chats, the author is present on Twitter to answer questions about the week's book. Hosted by The Nerdy Book Club's Donalyn Miller and Colby Sharp, #TitleTalk is an hour long Twitter chat that takes place the last Sunday of every month at 8 p.m. ET. The first half of the chat focuses on literacy topics and the second on recommending titles. These are just two of many venues on Twitter that connect teachers around the globe to promote reading and literacy. (See Chapter 4 for tips on starting a Twitter book club and Twitter chats among your students to promote reading and discussion of great books.)

BUILDING READING SKILLS WITH AUDIOBOOKS, READ-ALOUDS, AND PODCASTS

Reading practice is important for all readers, but so is *listening* practice. Based on the research on read-alouds (Layne, 2015), listening to quality reading helps struggling readers build vocabulary, comprehension, fluency, and reading skills; encourages listening skills; builds rapport between teacher and student; and promotes reading.

Beyond the traditional approach of reading the same book aloud to your entire class, online resources can help add listening practice to your students' day. From such sites as Audible, Google Play Books, or BookShout, you can download audiobooks for students to listen to for read-alouds, for small group work, or as an alternative to reading an entire book that is part of the curriculum. Although Audible, Google Play Books, and BookShout are paid sites, the free OverDrive and Hoopla apps enable you and your students to listen to ebooks checked out from your local or school library. In fact, I listen to books while driving to and from work to keep current with young adult literature (and other titles that I am interested in reading). For shorter texts, check out the Actively Learn and Wonderopolis reading platforms, both of which offer audio features.

Additional resources are also available for students with such language disabilities as dyslexia and dysgraphia so that they can listen to the audio books while reading to help visualize and comprehend. Learning Ally, for example, offers 80,000 books (searchable by grade level and Lexile level) for K–12 students, but there is a cost for membership. Bookshare, on the other hand, provides free audiobooks to people who have a diagnosed difficulty reading.

My school provides audiobooks through Learning Ally for any student with a program modification for audiobooks.

Podcasts are another audio text that you can use as a teaching tool for struggling readers. In addition to *The Yarn*, two NPR podcast series, *RadioLab* and *StoryCorps*, are excellent for educational purposes. *RadioLab* is primarily a nonfiction podcast with episodes centered on a question or theme related to science and philosophy.

RadioLab podcasts often include interviews with scientists and researchers to present multiple perspectives on a topic. The "Lucy" episode of *RadioLab*, for instance, tells the true story of a psychologist and his wife who adopted a chimpanzee as an experiment to see if she would become more human in the right environment. The podcast is compelling because of the different viewpoints in the interviews embedded throughout; it allows the listener to come to his or her own conclusions on the relationship among humans and animals. This podcast may be appealing to students who have read Katherine Applegate's *The One and Only Ivan* (2012), a fictionalized account of a real gorilla who lived in a cage for twenty-seven years as a mall attraction before being sent to live at Zoo Atlanta.

RADIOLAB "LUCY"

Whereas *RadioLab* podcasts run in hour-long, nonfiction episodes, *StoryCorps* offers a collection of short stories and interviews of everyday people talking about a specific theme or moment in time. The *StoryCorps* podcasts are five minutes or fewer and intended to share heartwarming stories and conversations in order to build connections and compassion. *StoryCorps* recording locations are available in four cities currently to record personal stories and words of wisdom, and you could easily adapt the concept to your classroom. Imagine providing your *StoryCorps*-style sound booth in your school or classroom for students to tell their stories in response to the stories they read. Additionally, you might get parents involved and ask families to respond to a shared text using Flipgrid, a closed video recording platform for students to verbally share insight and reflections.

My favorite podcast series is *The Tim Ferriss Show* on which Tim Ferriss interviews scientists, writers, and entrepreneurs. Due to mature language, it is not a podcast to share with students in its entirety, but excerpts from episodes can inspire and ignite a conversation or even lead to further reading and investigation. For example, in the episode "Lessons from Steve Jobs, Leonardo da Vinci, and Ben Franklin," Ferriss interviews Walter Isaacson, a Tulane University professor and author of biographies on Steve Jobs, Benjamin Franklin, and Leonardo da Vinci; listeners learn about the strengths and weaknesses of these three disparate inventors who helped shaped our history. Having students listen to parts of a podcast or reading pieces of a podcast transcript can be used for a reading and listening activity to compare and contrast, make predictions, and construct knowledge.

METACOGNITION AND APPS FOR THAT

Good readers monitor their understanding of a text as they read, recognize when the text has stopped making sense, and choose a strategy to employ to overcome the problem and achieve better understanding and clarity. This "knowing about knowing" or "thinking about one's thinking" is called *metacognition* and is a habit proficient readers utilize. When struggling readers are reading, they might just want to get to the end of the page or passage to be "done" and say they read the text. In actuality, however, they do not really understand what they just read so cannot use this information. They need to apply metacognition. When students are aware of their thinking and can articulate how they learn best, you can give them the necessary tools and strategies to help them get unstuck when reading becomes confusion.

Struggling readers often need help and practice with metacognition skills and employing strategies, such as those listed in the "Fix-It Strategies" sidebar. You can scaffold reading assignments with fix-it strategies in mind to help students check for understanding. Additionally, modeling and teaching readers these Fix-It strategies offers a toolbox of skills that students can access when they are struggling with a text. It is important to promote tenacity when supporting struggling readers, because you are then helping students think about what they can do when they get stuck in a text.

Struggling readers have different reasons for why they are struggling, so introducing them to a variety of metacognition strategies and technology tools will ultimately help them find the resources that will best help them fix the deficit. As teachers, it is up to us to provide the tools and help children narrow down which tools work best for them.

Text-to-speech tools can enable readers to listen to a text while they are reading along, which helps students build fluency in their own reading as well as supporting auditory learners. Wonderopolis and Actively Learn both enable students to listen to the text articles on their sites, for example. For text from

FIX-IT STRATEGIES

Cris Tovani (2000) identified twelve metacognition strategies that help readers foster better understanding of a text. While proficient readers may employ these instinctively, struggling readers need practice and support to master them. Offering struggling students a list of strategies, modeling with think-alouds, and practicing the strategies in class are helpful techniques to practice the habits of proficient readers and using metacognition. When readers encounter a difficult passage, encourage them to choose and use one or more of these fix-it strategies to help with reading comprehension:

- Go back and reread.
- Stop and think about what was read previously.
- Visualize.
- Read more to see if it becomes clear.
- Retell what you read aloud.
- Make a prediction.
- Slow down or skim the reading.

- Ask a question, and try to answer it.
- Reflect by writing about what you read.
- Make a connection between text and life, another text, or knowledge of the world.
- Notice patterns in text structure. (How is it organized? Does it help comprehension?) (Tovani, 2000, p. 6)

other sources, Voice Dream Reader, a paid app, reads PDF and Microsoft Word documents aloud, highlighting the text as it reads. This app is linked with Google Docs, Dropbox, and Bookshare. Whereas Voice Dream Reader reads print text, other text-to-speech apps depend on the user to dictate to the app. The app then plays back the dictated text while displaying it on screen, reinforcing the learning process through both sight and sound. The student can compare the dictated text to see if it visually matches the text he or she just read. Many of these apps require a few tries to learn the speaker's voice and correctly annotate the speaker's words before accurately playing back what was recorded. Recommended text-to-speech apps to support struggling readers include the free Chrome extension Speak It! and the paid app Dragon NaturallySpeaking.

When assigned a challenging text to read, older students can use Rewordify (Rewordify.com) to translate complicated English into simpler English. Students copy and paste or type a chunk of text into the site's translation box, and it translates the more difficult words. For a struggling reader who has to read a primary document in history or a complex chapter in a science textbook, Rewordify can help adjust the vocabulary for better understanding. Instead of becoming frustrated and abandoning the reading, students can use Rewordify as a scaffolds to help them make tough texts more accessible. Rewordify and similar technology tools are scaffolds to support and help students to comprehend and be actively engaged participants in classroom activities and discussions.

AS YOU GO FORWARD

Reading struggles spill over to affect many aspects of a student's education. A child having difficulty reading the content in reading class may struggle in social studies class, for example, not because the content is too challenging, but because the student has difficulty reading the required assignments. Rather than penalize the struggling reader, look for solutions. Many digital textbooks, for example, include a read-aloud feature that enables the struggling reader to learn the content by listening to the text. As Suzanne Carreker (2017) stated, "Reading proficiency is the key to academic success and economic opportunities, and time is of the essence where non-proficient adolescent readers are concerned" (p. 9). Instructional needs for struggling readers include consistent reading practice, scaffolding, and opportunities to listen to, independently read, and analyze text. The technology tools presented in this chapter offer supports and scaffolding for all types of readers, but benefit struggling readers in particular.

Empower your struggling readers to use various technologies that will help them achieve their personalized reading goals. Give struggling readers the opportunity to leverage technology so they can be in control of their own learning. Educators no longer need to be on top of students, coercing them to learn how to read. The idea of empowerment—giving students the technology, fix-it strategies, and choices that put them in control of the situation—is important for the struggling reader who wants to improve. You can empower them to work on their weaknesses and hone in on their strengths, as well as to believe they *can* become more proficient readers. In the next chapter, you'll learn how to encourage students who may have more developed reading skills but lack the incentive and tenacity to read.

TABLE 1.1 PAIRING TOOLS WITH TEACHING STRATEGIES

TEACHING STRATEGY (PEDAGOGY)	TECHNOLOGY TOOL	LINK
Matching students with the right text	DIBELS	dibels.uoregon.edu/assessment
	DRA	goo.gl/Pbrfzj
	Education Chats	goo.gl/obRbsR
	Goodreads	goodreads.com
	Lexile	Lexile.com
	The Nerdy Book Club	nerdybookclub.wordpress.com
	The Yarn	goo.gl/afGGwd
	#TitleTalk	titletalkchat.wordpress.com
	#2JennsBookClub	2jennsbookclub.com
Using audio tools and audiobooks	Audible	audible.com
	Bookshare	bookshare.org
	BookShout	bookshout.com
	Dragon NaturallySpeaking	nuance.com/dragon.html
	Flipgrid	flipgrid.com
	Google Play Books	play.google.com/books
	Hoopla	hoopladigital.com
	Learning Ally	learningally.org
	Overdrive	app.overdrive.com
	RadioLab	radiolab.org
	Speak It!	goo.gl/q0FGWp
	StoryCorps	storycorps.org
	The Tim Ferriss Show	tim.blog
	Voice Dream Reader	voicedream.com

COMMON CORE STATE STANDARDS	ISTE STANDARDS FOR STUDENTS AND FOR EDUCATORS
CCSS.ELA-Literacy.CCRA.R.10 Read and comprehend complex literary and informational texts independently and proficiently.	(E) 2. Leader Educators seek out opportunities for leadership to support student empowerment and success and to improve teaching and learning.
CCSS.ELA-Literacy.CCRA.R.7 Integrate and evaluate content presented in diverse media and formats, including visually and quantitatively, as well as in words.	(S) 1b. Empowered Learner Students build networks and customize their learning environments in ways that support the learning process.

continues on next page

TABLE 1.1   PAIRING TOOLS WITH TEACHING STRATEGIES, *CONTINUED*

TEACHING STRATEGY (PEDAGOGY)	TECHNOLOGY TOOL	LINK
Digital reading platforms for teaching reading and reading strategies	Actively Learn	activelylearn.com
	Newsela	newsela.com
	Wonderopolis	wonderopolis.org
Translating complex texts	Rewordify	rewordify.com

COMMON CORE STATE STANDARDS	ISTE STANDARDS FOR STUDENTS AND FOR EDUCATORS
CCSS.ELA-Literacy.CCRA.R.1 Read closely to determine what the text says explicitly and to make logical inferences from it; cite specific textual evidence when writing or speaking to support conclusions drawn from the text. CCSS.ELA-Literacy.CCRA.R.2 Determine central ideas or themes of a text and analyze their development; summarize the key supporting details and ideas.	(S) 1c. Empowered Learner Students use technology to seek feedback that informs and improves their practice and to demonstrate their learning in a variety of ways.
CCSS.ELA-Literacy.CCRA.R.10 Read and comprehend complex literary and informational texts independently and proficiently.	(S) 1. Empowered Learner Students leverage technology to take an active role in choosing, achieving, and demonstrating competency in their learning goals.

CHAPTER 2

RELUCTANT READERS

Have you ever tried to listen to a long, boring

schoolbook on a warm, lazy day? And have you ever

wondered why anyone would make a book so boring?

Then you are just like Alice.

—Jon Scieszka, *Walt Disney's Alice in Wonderland*

In middle school, *I* was the reluctant reader, starting books but then barely reading beyond a few pages. I knew *how* to read. I just didn't *care* to read. I would start a book, and then never finish reading cover to cover. My teachers, I was convinced, selected whole-class novels specifically to punish students. The plots of *Dicey's Song* (Voigt, 1982), *A Separate Peace* (Knowles, 1959), and *The Catcher in the Rye* (Salinger, 1951), were not adolescent experiences I could connect to, and grappling with the mathematical novella *Flatland* (Abbott, 1884) was like reading hieroglyphs (math was not my strong suit). Rather than fuel feeding the flames of my imagination, books were just dry stacks of paper. In college my love of books and reading finally ignited, and today as a middle school English teacher my passion is to encourage and support reluctant readers to overcome the same dissatisfaction with books that I once felt.

Reluctant readers may be struggling readers or simply students who have had negative experiences with reading. If reluctant readers aren't hooked on the first page of a book, they are quick to abandon it, like I was. Motivation and choice are key with reluctant readers. To help them, we educators must stop inadvertently committing "readicide" (Gallagher, 2009) and focus more on what Steven Wolk (2009) described as a "living curriculum" (p. 666), a place where students and teachers use books and other resources, as well as experience, to drive classroom inquiry. One of our goals as educators is developing critical thinking, stamina, and a life-long love of reading among our students.

To accomplish these goals for all the diverse readers in our classrooms, we must look up from the printed page and tap into all forms of text. As you will learn in this chapter, you can use visual texts—photographs, movies, and animated shorts—to pique the interest of reluctant readers, to enable them to build visual literacy, and to practice the strategies of proficient readers to perform a close read. Such visual texts can then serve as a bridge to print texts for reluctant readers. Once students are reading these images and visual texts, honing in on the "during reading" skills of making predictions and inferences helps keep students active as readers and can even drive them to finish the story. Students also need practice discerning the important parts of what they read in order to more effectively write or create responses to their reading. (See the "Strategies of Proficient Readers" section in the Introduction for a complete list of common skills.) Because they employ these skills and strategies, proficient readers excel at close reading. This chapter also will spotlight technology tools and curricular activities that can help students improve their visual literacy and movie making.

THE LAYERS OF A CLOSE READ

In their book *Close Reading and Writing from Sources* (2014), Douglas Fisher and Nancy Frey described a *close read* of a text as being composed of three layers of readings, each building on the next for deeper, or closer, understanding:

- ✦ **LAYER 1, FIRST READING.** Look at what the text says. This is the literal understanding of the text. When you ask students, "What is the gist of the text or story?" you are asking them to recall, summarize, and pull out the important details. By the time students are in middle school, this literal understanding is expected in the first read.

- ✦ **LAYER 2, SECOND READING.** Pay attention to "How does the text work?" This read is for craft, vocabulary (word choice), and structure. Take note of such aspects as literary devices, figurative language, poetic devices, and text structure. This can be more challenging for students if they do not know many literary devices. They may need support to uncover the metaphors, understand the imagery, or notice the emphasis of specific word choices or repetition the author uses.

- ✦ **LAYER 3, THIRD READING.** Ask, "What does the text mean?" This is the integration of knowledge and ideas, how a part of the text integrates with the whole text. In this reading students uncover the author's purpose, bias, mood, and tone, as well as make intertextual connections with the world outside the text (or text to text).

These layers of reading are challenging for most students, and reluctant readers especially. The more practice students have with these reading skills, the more they are able to build endurance with more challenging text. Through close reading and discussions of such visual texts as short films or photographs, you can show students not only how to use close reading and thinking skills, but also that they are using the same skills you expect them to apply to reading print text for school.

TEACHING READING WITH VISUAL TEXT

In Monica Hesse's historical novel of German-occupied Amsterdam, *Girl in the Blue Coat* (2016), the protagonist, sixteen-year-old Hanneke, looks at photographs for clues that might help her find a missing Jewish girl, and thinks, "Photographs...they tell a miniature story" (p. 195). Hanneke is right. Visual images say as much as printed text; sometimes photographs say even more because words can be limiting. Visual images are excellent resources to help practice the skills of close reading and engage reluctant readers.

In our everyday lives, print text merges with visual text on Facebook, Snapchat, Instagram, and other social media. As a result, students are reading more and more on screen than on paper and need to apply reading skills to visual media. Even the Common Core State Standards (CCSS) for Reading Grade 8 have taken into account visual texts as a tool to compare and contrast across texts, stating, "Analyze the extent to which a filmed or live production of a story or drama stays faithful to or departs from the text or script, evaluating the choices made by the director or actors" (CCSS.ELA-Literacy.RL.8.7). The key words here are *analyze* and *evaluate*; the CCSS are asking students to investigate and examine visual texts in the same way they investigate and interpret printed text.

As technology and a school's ability to integrate it continue to evolve, teachers must continue to support and equip students with literacy skills to read all texts closely and critically. This entails developing skills to read images and words in print and online, as well as to decode their messages, critically and closely. In the age of the Common Core State Standards, teachers are asking students to "mine the text for details, ideas, and deeper meanings" (Fisher and Frey, 2014). With printed text, this can be a challenge for many students, especially reluctant readers. Words have literal meanings and figurative meanings that can be challenging to unlock without practice. With images, the challenge of words is removed; students bring their own words to the text.

Photographs, short films, and movies can be used to practice the strategies of close reading. Films are a text and should be taught in a way that mirrors the way you teach close reading and critical thinking. Just as print text is layered with words, images, inferences, and evidence, so is film. When teaching with videos, as with printed text, model and scaffold to support your students so that they can, as Ziemke (2016) says, "interact, respond, and think to read the world differently" (p. 32). For many reluctant readers, stamina and commitment are required; practicing the habits of proficient readers with visual texts helps to build the reading muscles for these students.

VIEW NOW DO NOW

One resource that provides a visual literacy curriculum is The Jacob Burns Film Center (JBFC), a nonprofit cultural arts center dedicated to teaching literacy for a visual culture in Pleasantville, New York. On their website, you and your students can access a visual glossary of film terminology and short exercises called View Now Do Nows (**FIGURE 2.1**) to practice close-reading of images. Each day, the Jacob Burns Film Center website features one View Now Do Now, or you can search a library of almost 200 of these activities, filtering by concept.

VIEW NOW DO NOW

FIGURE 2.1 In View Now Do Now 179, students examine a still image from the movie *Hidden Figures* (2016), noting the artifacts in the scene that suggest the setting's time period.

Encouraging creativity and engagement with visual texts, View Now Do Nows are short reading and writing tasks for which students respond to a picture or film by making connections, telling a story, or thinking critically. Students can submit their responses by clicking the Respond Now button on the website, as well as see samples of other students' responses. View Now Do Nows address literacy concepts that mirror literature and text study: structure, mood, setting, character, theme, and style. While studying the photograph or film clip, students are using some of the same skills as when they read print text: infer, connect, evaluate, and summarize.

VIEW THREE TIMES

Using short animated films as a text also can help develop visual literacy skills and close reading strategies. When using short animated films in the classroom, follow Fisher and Frey's advice and have your students view the film three times. Students will be drawn to the text because they will think they are only watching a movie, but through discussion and rereading the film, you can show students that they are using close reading and thinking skills—the same they need to apply to a print text. During the first reading, have students view the film to get the gist and summarize the events in the text. In discussion, students can share other things they noticed in the film, what stood out, or caught their attention. The second time students watch the film, ask them to look at the craft of the film: the types of shots, as well as the use of colors, structure, and point of view. How do these elements shape the filmmaker's purpose and the central idea in the text? The third viewing can be done in small groups, independently, or as a whole class. The third viewing is the time to think about the use of sound and how it impacts the viewer: How do the images and sound affect the mood and tone in the film, and how do they confirm the central idea?

WHAT TO LOOK FOR WHEN READING AND VIEWING FILM

1. **FIRST VIEWING:** Get the gist of the story, make connections, and ask questions.

2. **SECOND VIEWING:** Look at the craft of the film, including the use of colors, structure, and point of view.

3. **THIRD VIEWING:** Pay attention to editing, symbolism, foreshadowing, and the like. Listen closely to music for more symbolism and foreshadowing.

TOOLS FOR VIEWING

When it comes to presenting films for your class to view, you have plenty of options. You can show a video or movie to the whole class, or flip the lesson and require students to view the movie before attending class. For a whole class lesson, you can share a short animated film and model your thinking and viewing of the film as if you were modeling a read-aloud of a picture book or a mentor text. For independent student practice, you can embed images and short films, along with instructions and response questions, into a digital assignment with Google Forms or Edpuzzle. Edpuzzle allows you to upload your own videos from YouTube, Khan Academy, or Vimeo and then include questions for before, during, and after a viewing to create an inter-active video assignment (**FIGURE 2.2**). Students answer the questions at their own pace to showcase their understanding, while you can track thinking and progress using Edpuzzle reports.

FIGURE 2.2
Viewing a clip, such as Atticus Finch's closing argument in the film *To Kill a Mockingbird* (1962), is interactive on Edpuzzle. Question mark icons identify questions that students must answer during and after viewing the clip.

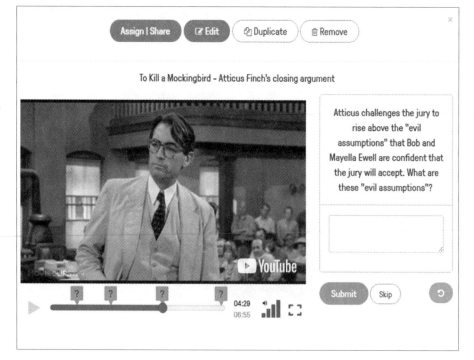

Viewing becomes more interactive, because students are not simply consuming videos but are articulating their thinking before, during, and after viewing the video content right in Edpuzzle. In content area classes, students can use Edpuzzle to view, for example, a science video or historical documentary for homework, responding to the questions embedded in the video as a check for understanding. Plus, students can watch a film or video as many times as they need to complete the questions and extract the key information for understanding. Teachers can search through the teacher-created content or customize their own interactive video viewing activities.

For elementary students and even ELL students, BrainPOP is a great source for videos, animations, and activities. BrainPOP provides informative animated content covering social studies, grammar, health, English, art, and music. A subscription to BrainPOP includes access to all the videos, worksheets and graphic organizers, games, and resources on the website. With BrainPOP, you use the content created in the platform, whereas Edpuzzle allows teachers to curate videos from different venues and personalize questions for understanding, making connections, comparing ideas, and evaluating information.

For middle and high school students, TED, which offers presentations and keynotes, is a good source for content videos that you can use to introduce a topic. For example, in the TEDxNextGeneration Talk, "What's Wrong with Our Food System? And How Can We Make a Difference?," eleven-year-old Birke Baehr (2010) passionately and persuasively talks about genetically modified foods (GMOs). You could use this video to kick off a lesson and spark a discussion or as a text for students to read and respond to. Or, pair this same video with excerpts from printed texts like *Chew on This: Everything You Don't Want to Know About Fast Food* (2007) by Charles Wilson and Eric Schlosser or Michael Pollan's *The Omnivore's Dilemma: The Secrets Behind What You Eat, Young Readers Edition* (2015).

For a different spin, Flocabulary offers videos using educational hip-hop songs to explain a wide variety of topics—from vocabulary and language

FIVE ANIMATED SHORTS TO USE IN THE CLASSROOM

If you're looking for story-driven text pairings with images and film, Vimeo and YouTube offer story-centered animations and live-action short films. Here are some of my favorites:

- *Piper* (2016)
- *The Present* (2014)
- *You Look Scary* (2016)
- *Alma* (2009)
- *The Blue Umbrella* (2013)

arts concepts, such as setting and hyperbole, to math and science concepts, such as geometry and the phases of the moon, to history and current events. Flocabulary offers free videos, or with a paid subscription, teachers can access more songs as well as lessons to coincide with them. Flocabulary can be used as part of a lesson or students can even create their own academic hip-hop songs about a particular topic, thereby meeting ISTE Standards for Students for Creative Communicator and Innovative Designer (2016).

PAIRING IMAGES WITH TEXT

PLASTIC BAG

Videos and photos can stand alone, and they can also be paired with print text to help students practice their critical reading and thinking skills across texts. Building text sets with films, articles, excerpts of literature, and poetry helps students to see and read a diversity of voices and perspectives about a specific subject. For example, for secondary-school students, you could start with viewing *Plastic Bag* (Spielberg & Bahrani, 2009), a twenty-minute film about pollution from the perspective of a plastic bag. Narrated by the actor Werner Herzog, the short film works well for teaching thematic ideas across content areas. For instance, you could make it the centerpiece of a lesson on point of view in English class or for studying global warming, pollution, and the environment in science class.

After viewing *Plastic Bag*, students could map the bag's journey on an inter-active Google map or write a story about a day in the life of an inanimate object of their choice. You could then pair the film with text readings related to the human impact on the environment, pollution, and the Earth, such as the *EcoWatch* (D'Alessandro, 2014) article "22 Facts About Plastic Pollution (And 10 Things We Can Do About It)."

ECOWATCH

Kwa Heri Mandima (2012) is another film that you can use with older students to teach story elements and point of view. A retrospective documentary, the film uses photographs and narration to describe what it's like to leave the only home you've known. Specifically, the film shares the memories of writer and director Robert-Jan Lacombe, who grew up in Zaire (now the Democratic Republic of the Congo) until age ten when he and his family flew back to Europe because of an impending civil war. The film is narrated in French with English subtitles, so students need to read the text of the film to understand the layers of meaning in the photographs. (This might be a challenge for some readers, including struggling readers.) Using the film without the narration is just as powerful; students can view the images then make predictions or write stories inspired by the images presented through-out the film. *Kwa Heri Mandima* is effective for teaching memoir, telling stories from photographs, and investigating themes of home, youth, and civil war in Zaire, now the Democratic Republic of the Congo. You could pair the film with such books as Ishmael Beah's *A Long Way Gone: Memoirs of a Boy Soldier* (2008) or Elie Wiesel's *Night* (2006); both are memoirs of young men who were prisoners of war far from the world they knew. Building text sets with diverse media including film, short stories, fiction, and nonfiction helps build critical viewers and digital learners.

KWA HERI MANDIMA

FILM AND VIDEO TO SYNTHESIZE UNDERSTANDING

Just as film and photographs can invite reluctant readers into a text, film and photographs can help them synthesize and evaluate a text. One method is to use the Five Frame Story activity from *Image, Sound, and Story*, the Jacob Burns

Film Center's visual literacy curriculum (**FIGURE 2.3**). Students read a story or text, then are tasked to summarize it in five pictures, or frames. Students cannot use words or captions to convey meaning, however, only images. Students first complete the storyboard to sketch their ideas, like a filmmaker. Then, you can extend this activity by having students use tablets or smartphones to take pictures that represent the key five scenes or pertinent ideas in the story. After students successfully convey the five pertinent ideas from the story, they can put the pictures together using Google Slides or a video creation app, such as Animoto. Students can work individually or in small groups.

FIVE FRAME STORY

Group _____   Date _____

TITLE

_____

_____

_____

Introduce a character or situation

Show a problem

CREATED BY _____

SHOT TYPE _____

ACTION _____

SOUND _____

SHOT TYPE _____

ACTION _____

SOUND _____

Show an attempt at a solution

Resolve the problem

Show the change in the character or situation

SHOT TYPE _____

ACTION _____

SOUND _____

SHOT TYPE _____

ACTION _____

SOUND _____

SHOT TYPE _____

ACTION _____

SOUND _____

ᴐ JACOB BURNS **FILM CENTER**

FIGURE 2.3 The Five Frame Story activity from the Jacob Burns Film Center challenges students to summarize a story or text in five images.

For example, I use a Five Frame Photo Stories assignment for a short story unit of study. At the culmination of reading a variety of short stories together, students are assigned to work in small groups; each group reads a different story and completes a five-frame storyboard, and creates images to bring the storyboard to life. The assignment requires students to show comprehension of the text, as well use images to convey the theme and characterization. Students share their Five Frame Photo Stories with the whole class, and we use them as a discussion springboard to help students look more closely at the text and peel back the layers of meaning.

STORYBOARDS, COMIC STRIPS, AND ANIMATIONS

Storyboarding and animation-creation platforms enable students to expand their evaluation, retelling, or interpretation of a story beyond five frames. Storyboard That is a digital storyboard creator for teachers and students to create and access storyboards of popular literature and historical events. On the free version, teachers can access the lesson plans and illustrated storyboards of popular literature and events in history. The free version allows you to create a six-cell storyboard. With the paid version, you can download the illustrated storyboards, create and customize storyboards with more than six cells, plus upload your own photos, record audio, and export to Google Slides or Microsoft PowerPoint. In addition, comic-strip-creation tools, such as Pixton, and animated video creators, such as PowToon, enable your students to create engaging visuals representing their understanding of a book or concept and then extend their thinking by adding captions and dialogue.

#BOOKSNAPS

Whereas students can use the previous tools to plot the key events of a story or create a visual story, with #BookSnaps they can merge words and pictures to showcase evidence of thinking about a text. According to educator and #BookSnaps creator Tara M. Martin,

#BookSnaps can be used to annotate and share excerpts of the book; showcase connections, an idea, or thought by creating a digital visual representation; diagram the rise, fall, and climax of the plot; highlight figurative language and imagery, notate character conflict, and internal struggles; and point out the main idea or a supporting argument. (Martin, 2016)

To create a #BookSnaps, students use the social media tool Snapchat to snap photos, combine them, type reflections on or interpretations of quotes, add stickers, and share the results with classmates. **FIGURE 2.4** is a #BookSnaps one of my students created. I use #BookSnaps as an introduction to annotating and coding the text. #BookSnaps lend themselves to conversations about what is important to highlight in the text versus what is interesting, and they showcase students thoughts, questions, reactions, and insight about their reading. Either way, the #BookSnaps allow students to show their thinking in and about the text.

FIGURE 2.4
Students create #BookSnaps to show thinking while reading by sharing personal responses, connections, and reactions to the text.

Girls (and boys) are held to unrealistic standards.

A female character must be likable above all else, lest she sacrifice the ideal.

Unfortunately, emotional pain and trauma contradict the primary Sugar and Spice tenets of Being a Girl. Nothing about pain is *likable*. It's often harsh, selfish, all-consuming, alienating, loud and ugly. A girl in pain can be all of these things at once, but if she is, that means she certainly sacrifices the ideal, and let's face it: a girl who isn't nice isn't nice to read *about*.

Everyone has emotions. Many times people are told to suppress their emotions. Suppressing emotions can often lead to "increased physical stress on your body, including high blood pressure, increased incidence of diabetes and heart disease"

AS YOU GO FORWARD

When reluctant students are given a text, if it is too easy or too difficult, the student can shut down. Using photos and film takes the first challenge away by eliminating the words. Students are able to put their own words into the text to articulate and annotate it. This gradual release into the text builds background knowledge and understanding before words are read on a page. Then, through interactive lessons, discussions, and close reading exercises, photographs and images become a bridge to help reluctant readers see the depth and pleasure of text.

TABLE 2.1   PAIRING TOOLS WITH TEACHING STRATEGIES

TEACHING STRATEGY (PEDAGOGY)	TECHNOLOGY TOOLS	LINKS
Using visual texts to teach reading strategies	Animoto	animoto.com
	#BookSnaps	goo.gl/eFaFnx
	BrainPOP	brainpop.com
	Edpuzzle	edpuzzle.com
	Flocabulary	flocabulary.com
	Google Forms	google.com/forms
	Google Slides	google.com/slides
	iMovie	apple.com/imovie
	Jacob Burns Film Center: View Now Do Nows	goo.gl/yu9NzC
	Khan Academy	khanacademy.org
	Pixton	pixton.com
	PowToon	powtoon.com
	Storyboard That	storyboardthat.com
	Vimeo	vimeo.com
	YouTube	youtube.com

COMMON CORE STATE STANDARDS	ISTE STANDARDS FOR STUDENTS AND FOR EDUCATORS
CCSS.ELA-Literacy.CCRA.R.1	(E) 5a. Designer
Read closely to determine what the text says explicitly and to make logical inferences from it; cite specific textual evidence when writing or speaking to support conclusions drawn from the text.	Use technology to create, adapt, and personalize learning experiences that foster independent learning and accommodate learner differences and needs.
CCSS.ELA-Literacy.CCRA.R.2	
Determine central ideas or themes of a text and analyze their development; summarize the key supporting details and ideas.	
CCSS.ELA-Literacy.RL.8.7	
Analyze the extent to which a filmed or live production of a story or drama stays faithful to or departs from the text or script, evaluating the choices made by the director or actors.	

CHAPTER 3

ENGLISH LANGUAGE LEARNERS

The first thing I learned that day was this:

what you think you know about a person is

only a fraction of the story.

—Gavin Extence, *The Universe Versus Alex Woods*

English language learners (ELL, also called English learners) are as diverse in their skill levels as any other group of readers. Entering school speaking a variety of languages and with varying degrees of English abilities, students who are English language learners work double time to simultaneously understand the language and content-specific lessons. Meeting all these students' needs requires creativity, differentiation, and personalization.

Technology tools can help ELL students meet the demands of the curriculum and build understanding so they can meet learning objectives. As authors Heather Parris, Lisa Estrada, and Andrea Honigsfeld (2017) explained in *ELL Frontiers: Using Technology to Enhance Instruction for English Learners,*

> *The use of digital media provides a low-anxiety environment with a focus on the traditional four language skills (listening, speaking, reading, writing), plus the skill of viewing, which must be included in today's classroom. ELs need ample production opportunities to develop language skills"* (p. 26).

This chapter delves into the wealth of technology tools and diverse teaching strategies available to you to support ELL students in developing their language skills. You'll learn about online visual curation tools for building vocabulary, mind-mapping tools to scaffold information, and more. Finally, you'll take a virtual field trip through virtual reality (VR) and augmented reality (AR) tools as a way to build background knowledge and vocabulary.

TRANSLATE, SAY LESS, AND SCAFFOLD

Although Google Translate is just a click away, it isn't always the best choice to help bridge the language gap for ELL students. It is not always accurate, especially not for translating chunks of text or a whole text in a student's first language. (In fact, it was an ELL student who pointed this out to me.) Look beyond Google Translate, however, and you'll find many ways to support English language learners in your classroom.

Understanding a text is the vital first step in students being able to complete school assignments and participate in discussions about that text. Enabling students to use translators and dictionaries—whether electronic translators, paperback dictionaries, or smartphone apps—to translate content-specific vocabulary words into their primary language is important. Allowing students to read texts in their home language or on a lower Lexile level is also beneficial for ELL students. If possible, you could even acquire copies of required readings in students' home languages to aid comprehension and understanding of the content. My school, for instance, purchased copies of two required texts, Lois Lowry's *The Giver* (1993) and Harper Lee's *To Kill a Mockingbird*, in Japanese and Spanish for students to borrow during an all-grade read. Additionally, offering bilingual texts and glossaries validate a student's home language. Graphic novel versions and video productions can also help students understand a story in an unfamiliar language. (Even native English speakers sometimes appreciate this approach for Shakespeare's plays.)

Finally, online reading platforms, such as Actively Learn and Newsela discussed in Chapter 1, enable ELL students to translate text into their home language to help overcome difficult vocabulary. Additionally, Actively Learn allows you to insert textual notes to support student understanding and define words within a passage. Students can also use the audio feature to read along with a text so that they hear the pronunciation of words they see. Focus on student understanding first, then help to build their speaking and writing skills.

When composing text-dependent comprehension questions for ELL students, saying less and saying it in simple and direct English is beneficial. Make sure that the words you use are ones your ELL students will understand. When asking ELL students about key ideas and details in *The Giver,* I say "List the rules where Jonas lives," for example. Rather than ask ELL students to compare and contrast the protagonist and his friend, I use simplified language: "Who is Asher? How is Asher like and different from Jonas?"

To help with writing prompts, provide a word bank and sometimes sentence stems for your ELL students. As an example, **FIGURE 3.1** shows a short response that I scaffolded for my ELL students so they could better understand

and complete a writing prompt for *To Kill a Mockingbird*. The original prompt asked,

> *What is the fundamental principle, rule of conduct, or law of life that Atticus is trying to communicate to his children? How does Atticus demonstrate the law of life that he expressed in the above quote? Use* **two** *examples from* To Kill a Mockingbird *to support your response.*

For someone learning English, that would be a very daunting assignment. Instead, rephrasing the short response question more simply and providing supports guides students through the writing assignment and helps them to articulate their thinking about the text. Dividing text into manageable chunks, such as breaking down a challenging paragraph into sentences for example, allows students to paraphrase and find meaning without getting overwhelmed. Providing students with a graphic organizer, such as Figure 3.1, then helps them record their paraphrasing and also requires them to identify and define key words. The first part of the revised prompt asks students to restate their understanding of the questions as a check for understanding: Do you know what you are being asked to write? The graphic organizer portion requires students to jot down their ideas in preparation for the answer. Finally, the sentence starters not only help students to put ideas down on paper, but also illustrate the format for writing this type of response. Scaffolding techniques that chunk the text, provide word banks, and ask students to create a visual representation can benefit students with various reading and writing weaknesses, while enabling you to assess their understanding and reading ability.

Before students complete a written response, supplementing the main text with images, word banks, and visual texts can help support ELL students' understanding. When my class begins reading *To Kill A Mockingbird*, for instance, I immerse students in the historical context through images, vocabulary words, and visual texts to help them all understand the socioeconomic, race, and gender implications within the text. Background knowledge regarding U.S. history and social customs is especially important to ELL students, who often come from very different cultural heritages and education experiences.

"You never really understand a person until you consider things from his point of view [...]
until you climb into his skin and walk around in it." (p. 33)

SHORT RESPONSE QUESTION

What does Atticus mean? How does he follow his own advice? Use two examples in *To Kill a Mockingbird* to show how he does this.

In your own words, restate the question and list the two requirements of the prompt.

QUESTION PART 1: _____

_____

_____

QUESTION PART 2: _____

_____

Answer the Question	Cite an example in the book Example #1	Explain how the example shows Atticus following his own advice Example #1
	Cite an example in the book Example #1	Explain how the example shows Atticus following his own advice Example #2

Now Let's Write Your Response—Use the sentence starters to help you.

When Atticus says _____,

he means _____.

Atticus follows his own advice when he _____.

In the text it states, " _____

_____ (pg.___)

This shows _____

Additionally, when Atticus _____

he is _____.

This is clear when the text says, " _____

_____ (pg.___)

These two examples show that Atticus is _____

and he _____.

FIGURE 3.1 A scaffolded writing prompt like this one for *To Kill a Mockingbird* can guide ELL students to more easily convey their thoughts on a subject.

VISUAL CURATION TOOLS FOR UNDERSTANDING

As you learned in Chapter 2, photographs, images, and films are great tools for supporting student learning and understanding. Visuals are universal in many ways because an image is a sign that students recognize, when words might be challenging, complex, or confusing. For ELL students especially, visual references are beneficial in building content-specific vocabulary. ELL students might not have the language proficiency, but that does not mean they are not full of knowledge. Graphic organizers, such as Frayer Models (**FIGURE 3.2**), enable students to define vocabulary words plus include synonyms and visual references to help build their word knowledge. A definition is not enough to help students learn, understand, and apply vocabulary words. Students need to see, hear, read, and interact with words to help recognize, utilize, and understand new word knowledge.

FIGURE 3.2
Frayer Model activities help students build definitions of vocabulary words and concepts, including adding an illustration or sketch to help visualize the word meaning.

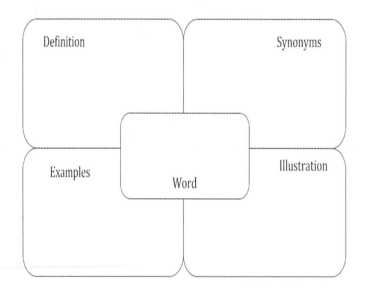

When teachers use graphic organizers for building word understanding, ELL students can collect these graphic organizers to build personalized, content-specific dictionaries that will help expand their understanding of the English language. Similarly, including photos and graphics for visual reference in word journals can also create custom dictionaries for ELL students.

Some teachers have students create sections in their notebooks to curate new vocabulary words, and students can also have a specific word journal to keep vocabulary words in one place. My high school geometry teacher, for example, required students to keep a separate journal with geometry vocabulary words, definitions, and drawings to help prepare for the tests (**FIGURE 3.3**).

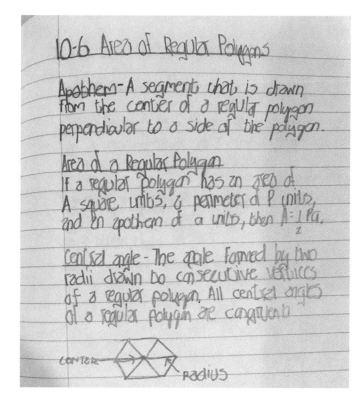

FIGURE 3.3 A vocabulary journal enables English language learners to keep content-specific vocabulary words in one place.

QUIZLET, THINGLINK, AND SYMBALOOEDU

Several technology tools enable teachers and students to build content-specific dictionaries online, as well. For example, Quizlet enables teachers and students alike to make digital flashcards sets. Students can create their own flashcard sets, or you can create a set to share with students for review. Quizlet's diagram feature enables teachers and students to create study diagrams with images and terminology to study and review materials. ELL and struggling students can use Quizlet Learn, along with the digital flashcards, to create a longer-term study plan to master concepts and vocabulary, as well.

With visual curation tools, such as ThingLink or SymbalooEDU, you and your students can build interactive text and image resources about specific topics or themes. For instance, the basic free educator membership for ThingLink allows you to create a ThingLink board and embed such content as video, slide shows, documents, and audio in and around the image. When studying vocabulary, for example, you or your students can upload an image to represent the vocabulary word, and then, to demonstrate the word's meaning add links with photos, videos, a sentence using the word, webpages, and even an audio clip of how to pronounce the word (**FIGURE 3.4**). With a paid subscription, you can access or upload 360-degree images, as well.

FIGURE 3.4 ThingLink boards, such as this one created for Chapter 1 of *The Giver*, can help students understand vocabulary.

SymbalooEDU, like ThingLink, allows you to create interactive content on a themed SymbalooEDU board and curate links to additional information. In my Speech and Debate class, for instance, I assigned students to create a board that answered the question: What makes a great speaker? The SymbalooEDU board had to contain videos of great speakers or links to famous speeches (**FIGURE 3.5**). Additionally, students were to include articles and interviews on the topic of effective public speaking. This assignment required the students to create their own boards to share with their peers; you can also create boards for resources and links to help students understand a concept or idea. SymbalooEDU can be utilized as a road map for lessons, activities, and flipped learning by linking tiles on a board to documents in Google Forms, videos, and digital activities for students to complete and show what they know. SymbalooEDU boards can be lessons themselves or for support materials and study guides for ELL and struggling students.

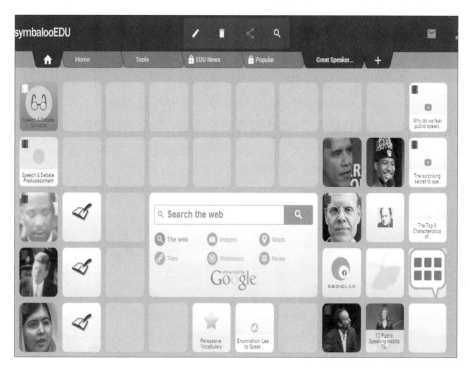

FIGURE 3.5
SymbalooEDU boards, such as this one on the theme "Great Speakers are Made, Not Born," can include videos, web links, texts, and more.

All these digital tools feature collaborative aspects that allow students to construct and curate information. You can have students work together, for instance, sharing images and links about a concept or theme, such as westward expansion. A SymbalooEDU board with links to content-specific vocabulary or root words, suffixes, and prefixes can be a good resource for ELL students to help each other build word knowledge and understand vocabulary in context. Likewise, a SymbalooEDU board on a specific place or time period with links to videos, images, print texts can be a helpful tool to provide context and enhance comprehension when studying a topic. When students create their own Quizlet flashcards or SymbalooEDU or ThingLink boards to help curate information, they are becoming Knowledge Creators and Empowered Learners (ISTE Standards for Students, 2016).

Digital tools can be used beyond vocabulary instruction. To show understanding of a history concept or a story, students can use cartoon platforms like Storyboard That and PowToon to create digital cartoons, merging images and words to communicate ideas, tell a story, and summarize a text. Students can storyboard the sequence of a short story or create a visual timeline of events in history, as well.

GRAPHIC ORGANIZERS AND CONCEPT MAPPERS

Digital graphic organizers like Popplet and Bubbl.us allow students to build concept maps and organize information. Sketchboard is another graphic organizer or concept-mapping tool that lets students sketch drawings, shapes, and people, plus utilize the icons provided on the platform to represent ideas. The sketches can be freehand or images and shapes provided in Sketchboard's library. With all three of these digital graphic organizers, users can collaborate on a sketch so a small group of students can share ideas to build a concept map to plot out textual examples to support a theme in a text, illustrate a characterization, or make a timeline. Whether students are creating a character chart in literature or illustrating the key concepts of mitosis, these digital tools can help them catalog and curate information. Utilizing these concept mapping and storyboard tools helps scaffold student thinking and understanding. In addition, these tools can help students formulate their thinking for a writing task.

Most importantly for this chapter, these support tools help ELL students to leverage learning, reinforce vocabulary, and build background knowledge. When you provide links and supplemental information, you enhance clarity. Not every student is going to look up words and information that they do not know, but when teachers provide these resources for their ELL students, they enhance understanding. These technology tools and teaching strategies help English language learners, as well as all learners, facilitating content and additional inferential knowledge.

SPEAKING AND LISTENING TO SHOW UNDERSTANDING OF READING

Speaking is one of the core literacy skills, but ELL students might be shy or overwhelmed to participate in a large class discussion because of their language skills. Initiating small groups discussions and one-on-one discussions is a way for students to share thinking, questions, connections, and synthesis of a text, while at the same time building language and speaking skills. Doing so also addresses Common Core State Standards, which require students initiate and participate in a range of collaborative discussions (CCSS. ELA-Literacy.SL.9-10.1). To help ELL students develop academic language, consider having students respond orally to a text using a technology tool, such as Flipgrid or Seesaw. Both sites remove the stress of performance in front of the class and give students the opportunity to present knowledge and ideas orally while building verbal communication.

FLIPGRID

With Flipgrid, you pose a question (or choose one of the ready-made prompts) for which students can record responses. You set the amount of time that students have to respond to a question; for example, students have one minute to answer a question or ninety seconds. Students can listen to each other's reflections to learn from them and respond to one another. Flipgrid also offers stickers, similar to those on Snapchat, for students to digitally accessorize their look on camera. For students who don't like to show their face on camera, you could keep a collection of masks or selfie props on hand for students to use when sharing on Flipgrid or any video sharing tool. Flipgrid is accessible in free or paid versions, but you must sign up for an account to access it. I've used Flipgrid for my students to share goals for the year at the start school, reflections after a field trip, and book reviews.

SEESAW

Similarly, the Seesaw app allows students to respond and reflect on a lesson or activity, but goes a step beyond just video and audio. On Seesaw, students can add written reflections and draw their responses. Students have more options for how they might share and reflect by adding a drawing to explain their thinking or their steps for solving a math problem. Students can view each other's written responses and add peer feedback with the app.

GOOD NETIQUETTE

Students' providing peer feedback with Seesaw, or any of the other video tools, however, raises the topic of digital citizenry. Be sure to have conversations with students about responsibility when posting online, even in closed educational platforms, such as Flipgrid and Seesaw. For some tips on starting the conversation, see **FIGURE 3.6**.

	Digital Citizen 101	What to Say . . . Sentence Stems
1.	Never give out personal information	I already know . . .
2.	Think before you post; write down what you are going to say before you say anything	This reminds me . . .
3.	Share your ideas and thoughts	I understand . . .
4.	Be positive	I am wondering . . .
5.	Speak clearly, slowly, and loud enough for your audience to hear you	

FIGURE 3.6
When your students are posting online, offer them some tips for being a good digital citizen.

BUILDING BACKGROUND KNOWLEDGE WITH VIRTUAL FIELD TRIPS

Benjamin Franklin's famous quote, "Tell me, and I forget. Teach me, and I remember. Involve me, and I learn," resonates especially true with ELL students. With telling and teaching, language can be a stumbling block that impedes understanding. Earlier in the chapter, I mentioned that saying less while making sure directions are clear and concise is beneficial for ELL students. Additionally, using visuals, in particular virtual reality, can help develop language and understanding for these students. An exciting way to remove that block while helping to build knowledge and introduce information in an interactive way is with virtual-reality (VR) and augmented-reality (AR) field trips, which offer students an interactive, three-dimensional learning experience. With virtual field trips, no walls divide the learning spaces, and students can experience outer space, explore museums and laboratories, and visit the world's natural wonders without leaving their classrooms.

VR field trips take the form of immersive 360-degree videos and are often viewed through headsets that look like a cross between a stereoscope and a smartphone, although some can be experienced through viewing on a tablet or laptop (see the sidebar, "Look Around"). Students can move the viewer up, down, and side-to-side to look around them, just as if they were in the scene. AR experiences are viewed on smartphones or tablets and feature 3D animations and videos superimposed on the students' surroundings. Again, by moving the viewer, students can see the animated objects from all angles.

Besides being a lot of fun, VR and AR field trips also enable teachers to design "authentic learner-driven activities and environments that recognize and accommodate learner variability" (ISTE Standards for Educators, 2017). Virtual Reality deepens learning by, for example, offering a visual tour through a coral reef where students are explorers. Additionally, some teachers are now having students create their own tours to share with the class. These do not just have to be 3D movies; with TimeLooper, a "time travel" app, students can examine history as if they were part of it, feeling like they have been taken back to the Great Fire of London in 1666, for example. With teacher planning and thought, these experiences can be used for classroom discussion, proposing solutions to such issues as global warming and pollution, or examining history and making connections with our lives today.

VIRTUAL CONTENT

Virtual, experiential learning experiences are available from a growing number of outlets. The Smithsonian Museum of Natural History, for example, is one of many museums to offer virtual tours of their exhibits that you can view on any device. *The New York Times* also offers a free VR smartphone app called NYT VR and a selection of 360-degree videos on science, current events, landmarks, and more. Specifically targeting the educational market, Discovery Education offers a broad selection of free VR experiences on its website, as well as coordinating lessons and webinars to help teachers get started with virtual field trips. The leader in the field, however, is Google with

LOOK AROUND

When talking about the hardware needed for virtual reality, there a many options. Immersive VR headsets are available as classroom kits through companies such as Best Buy or Dynamic Innovative Data Solutions. These kits are customizable and include student devices, virtual-reality viewers, chargers, routers, and a case or charging cart in a bundled price. Some virtual-reality glasses or viewers include sound for a full sensory effect. For less expensive VR viewers, Google Cardboard Kits and viewers are available at a fraction of the price; at this writing, Amazon was offering them for less than ten dollars a viewer. Some VR apps can be used with a smartphone on its own, but students would need to download the apps. Still another alternative to experience a virtual field trip is to use a class set of iPads or tablets equipped with the appropriate apps.

its Expeditions and Expeditions AR, which are "collections of virtual reality panoramas—360° panoramas and 3-D images—annotated with details, points of interest, and questions" (Google, 2016). The more than 500 Expedition experiences—from explorations of history and culture to scientific units of study covering marine life, space, geography, and more—are designed to be viewed using a Google Cardboard viewer and a smartphone. Immersed in the experience, students are the explorers and the teacher is the guide and facilitator.

NEARPOD

Designed to be a broader-use educational platform, Nearpod also offers over 350 ready-to-teach VR lessons, field trips, and 3D objects that can be viewed on smartphones, tablets, or laptops. You can use the ready-made lesson plans provided on Nearpod (exact content available depends on whether you're using the free version or one of the subscription options), or you can create your own interactive lessons with embedded quizzes, videos, drawings, slide presentations, and discussion boards. The self-paced lessons or teacher-led lessons allow students to work at their own speed and can offer scaffolded materials to support diverse student learners. A colleague of mine uses Nearpod's virtual field trips to enable her tenth-grade AP Global Studies class to virtually tour Angkor Wat in Cambodia via their smartphones and Chromebooks from Rye, New York. The tour of this religious temple allows students to be virtual anthropologists and see the grand size and materials used to build the temple, examining and developing questions about the ancient Khmer Empire and Cambodia.

BENEFITS BEYOND BOOKS

Whereas a chapter in a textbook or a collection of photos limits what students hear, see, and understand, using virtual reality enables students to move around and view their surroundings, and experience a place for themselves rather than through a writer or photographer's impressions. Students can then describe in their own words the breathtaking landscape around the world, underwater, and even in outer space, as well as apply this information to activities and readings for content learning.

Virtual field trips are scaffolding opportunities to help students, especially ELL students, make sense of larger concepts and ideas that might be difficult to read in a textbook or content-specific texts. Yvonne and David Freeman wrote in *Academic Language for English Language Learners and Struggling Readers* (2009), "Content area teachers need to help students develop the appropriate language for their subject through carefully scaffolded instruction" (p. 50). Taking VR field trips, promoting student talk and conversation, and offering writing opportunities after the experience can help ELL and struggling readers to build their academic language proficiency and their knowledge of the content material.

For example, while reading Malala Yousafzai's memoir, *I Am Malala* (2013), students could access *Clouds Over Sidra*, a story-based VR experience from

WITHIN, to parallel the displacement of many Syrians with the displaced people in Swat Valley, Pakistan. In *Clouds Over Sidra,* 12-year-old Sidra guides viewers through her temporary home and daily life in Jordan's Zaatari Refugee Camp. Students can see the landscape around her as she talks about her desire to go back home. These VR experiences help students build the important background knowledge, as well as make connections and comparisons that can motivate and engage them in their reading.

As Freeman and Freeman (2009) stated, "It is important for teachers to activate or build the background students will need to read a content text. Often teachers assume that ELL students have knowledge that, in fact, they were never exposed to....Without the appropriate background, text passages are very hard to understand" (p. 87). VR field trips enable students to immerse themselves in a learning experience, to become involved in the content, as Franklin recommended, rather just be told the facts. Virtual reality and augmented reality take collaboration to the next level, with students connecting, engaging, exploring, and examining remote destinations from multiple viewpoints to broaden their understanding and learning.

AS YOU GO FORWARD

English language learners are a diverse group of learners that often struggle because of a limited academic vocabulary and background knowledge. Technology can be a valuable resource for teachers to provide instruction and support for these students whom English is not their first language. It is challenging for secondary ELL students because they are learning English while filling in the gaps of missing content knowledge and academic vocabulary to succeed in school. Such technology tools as digital graphic organizers, audio and visual tools, and virtual reality provide scaffolds and support to introduce content and also create personalized learning opportunities to keep these learners actively engaged. Immersing students in literacy instruction that is meaningful and student-centered can enhance language instruction, help ELL students interact in the classroom more authentically, and provide content area support.

TABLE 3.1 PAIRING TOOLS WITH TEACHING STRATEGIES

TEACHING STRATEGY (PEDAGOGY)	TECHNOLOGY TOOLS	LINKS
Using graphic organizers to highlight the important parts of the text	Bubbl.us Popplet Sketchboard	bubbl.us popplet.com sketchboard.io
Summarizing information	Animoto GoAnimate PowToon Storyboard That	animoto.com goanimate.com powtoon.com storyboardthat.com
Building vocabulary with cultural connections and real-world interactions	Quizlet SymbalooEDU ThingLink	quizlet.com symbalooedu.com thinglink.com
Discussing books and having conversations about reading	Flipgrid Seesaw Skype	info.flipgrid.com web.seesaw.me skype.com

COMMON CORE STATE STANDARDS	ISTE STANDARDS FOR STUDENTS AND FOR TEACHERS
CCSS.ELA-Literacy.CCRA.R.7 Integrate and evaluate content presented in diverse media and formats, including visually and quantitatively, as well as in words	**(S) 3c. Knowledge Constructor** Students curate information from digital resources using a variety of tools and methods to create collections of artifacts that demonstrate meaningful connections or conclusions.
CCSS.ELA-Literacy.CCRA.R.2 Determine central ideas or themes of a text and analyze their development; summarize the key supporting details and ideas.	**(S) 3c. Knowledge Constructor** Students curate information from digital resources using a variety of tools and methods to create collections of artifacts that demonstrate meaningful connections or conclusions.
CCSS.ELA-Literacy.L.8.6 Acquire and use accurately grade-appropriate general academic and domain-specific words and phrases; gather vocabulary knowledge when considering a word or phrase important to comprehension or expression.	**(S) 3d. Knowledge Constructor** Students build knowledge by actively exploring real-world issues and problems, developing ideas and theories and pursuing answers and solutions.
CCSS.ELA-Literacy.CCRA.SL.1 Prepare for and participate effectively in a range of conversations and collaborations with diverse partners, building on others' ideas and expressing their own clearly and persuasively.	**(S) 6. Creative Communicator** Students communicate clearly and express themselves creatively for a variety of purposes using the platforms, tools, styles, formats, and digital media appropriate to their goals.

continues on next page

TABLE 3.1   PAIRING TOOLS WITH TEACHING STRATEGIES, *CONTINUED*

TEACHING STRATEGY (PEDAGOGY)	TECHNOLOGY TOOLS	LINKS
Building background knowledge with virtual field trips	Discovery Education	discoveryeducation.com
	Dynamic Innovative Data Solutions	didatasolutions.com
	Google Expeditions	edu.google.com/expeditions
	Google Expeditions Kits	goo.gl/UGsvkq
	Nearpod	nearpod.com
	NMNH Virtual Tour	naturalhistory.si.edu/vt3
	NYT VR	nytimes.com/marketing/nytvr
	Oculus	goo.gl/tHVo2L
	TimeLooper	timelooper.com
	WITHIN	with.in

COMMON CORE STATE STANDARDS	ISTE STANDARDS FOR STUDENTS AND FOR TEACHERS
CCSS.ELA-Literacy.CCRA.R.7	(S) 3d. Knowledge Constructor
Integrate and evaluate content presented in diverse media and formats, including visually and quantitatively, as well as in words.	Students build knowledge by actively exploring real-world issues and problems, developing ideas and theories and pursuing answers and solutions.

CHAPTER 4

ADVANCED READERS

Sometimes you read a book and it fills you with this weird evangelical zeal, and you become convinced that the shattered world will never be put back together unless and until all living humans read the book.

—John Green, *The Fault in Our Stars*

Advanced readers and gifted readers need to be challenged in the classroom, but that does not necessarily mean simply giving these students more work in the form of time fillers like crossword puzzles and word searches. Advanced readers need differentiated curriculum that meets their learning needs. This chapter will address ways to support advanced readers and create learning opportunities that challenge their higher-level reading abilities, thinking, comprehension, and questioning skills. Later in the chapter, you'll learn how to put the students at the forefront as discussion leaders and creators via Twitter book chats, an excellent tool for small groups to build conversations about reading and critical thinking. Advanced students are keen critical thinkers and many already "communicate clearly and express themselves creatively using technology platforms" (ISTE Standards for Students, 2016). As you'll see, allowing advanced readers to take the lead with Twitter book clubs and chats empowers them, enables them to leverage technology, and engages them in taking an active role in choosing, achieving, and demonstrating competency in their learning goals (ISTE, 2016).

CHALLENGING WORK VERSUS MORE WORK

Advanced students are not looking to complete more work but want learning experiences that challenge, push, and grow their thinking. Tiering assignments and offering differentiated choice menus (see Chapter 5) not only enables you to respond to different learning styles, but also to scaffold learning, increase challenge, foster intrinsic motivation, and offer variety to reach more students. A colleague of mine levels his math class work: Mustard, Wasabi, and Naga Jolokia (also known as ghost pepper). Mustard problems are at grade level, while Wasabis have some challenge. Naga Jolokia indicates advanced math and brainteasers above grade level for his students who are seeking more of a challenge. The tiered assignments allow students to select the level of challenge they want and complete the work that meets their abilities, while highlighting their strengths, and challenging their weaknesses to build skills.

When designing choice menus with questions to support advanced readers that tap into higher-order thinking, use Bloom's Taxonomy and Gardner's Multiple Intelligences as your guide. When you design independent projects based on student choice, higher-order questioning, and different learning styles, you enable advanced learners to explore personal areas of interest, sometimes going above and beyond what is covered in the curriculum.

A ROLL OF THE DICE

Traditional cubing or roll-the-dice activities are two differentiated activities that meet all students' needs. With a little customization, they can offer even more challenge for advanced readers. For example, when I am organizing an activity to check for reading understanding, I offer two options of discussion questions. Titled "I Read It, and I Understood What I Read," one version includes higher-order thinking questions for advanced students or students who want to be challenged. The second option, "I Read It, but I Didn't Totally Get It" has questions that are a mixture of low- and high-order thinking. **FIGURE 4.1** illustrates this approach in an assignment for small group discussion work after reading specific chapters in *To Kill a Mockingbird*. The questions are classified according to Bloom's Taxonomy Questions.

The questions and activities are printed on each side of a single page so that students can preview all the questions and complete those that are the best fit to build knowledge, understanding, and synthesis. The questions are coded to Bloom's Questioning Stems to show students that the higher numbers equate with more challenging questions but all levels are important for complex and deep understanding. Tiering the assignment this way allows for students to work at different levels of complexity and thinking. Because this is a roll-the-dice or cubing activity, students complete the questions they roll. Students can work in small groups or with a partner taking turns and collaborating on the more challenging questions.

A ROLL OF THE DICE

Level: "I Read It, but I Didn't Totally Get It"

TKAM Chapters 14–17 Comprehension/Analysis

NUMBER	TYPE OF THINKING	
1	Inference	Create a T chart for Dolphus Raymond. Record the rumors about Mr. Raymond on one side of the chart and what the children learn about Mr. Raymond talking and interacting with him outside of the courthouse. What inferences can be made about the type of person **Dolphus Raymond** is?
2	Comprehension	Read pages **223-227. List the 3 most IMPORTANT facts** that are revealed from the testimony of Heck Tate. Focus on **what Atticus feels Heck Tate failed to do** in one of your facts.
3	Application	**Draw** a picture of Tom Robinson based on the description from the middle of page 248 to the middle of page 249.
4	Analysis	Dissect Mr. Ewell's testimony (pages 227-238). **Create a table in which you record 2 of Mr. Ewell's direct quotes and state what the reader learns about his personality from each quote.**
5	Synthesis	Read the middle of page 228. Compare and contrast the description of the one corner of the Ewell's yard with the rest of the yard. **You may use words or draw a picture.**
6	Synthesis	How does Bob Ewell explain to Atticus why he did not call a doctor to examine Mayella? What is Atticus implying by asking both Heck Tate and Bob Ewell this question? What other details in Bob Ewell's description of the incident are most important to Atticus?

FIGURE 4.1A Differentiated roll-the-dice discussion questions like these let students choose to their pace. They can work at a more supportive pace.

A ROLL OF THE DICE

Level: "I Read It, and I Understood What I Read"

TKAM Chapters 14–17 Comprehension/Analysis

NUMBER	TYPE OF THINKING	
1	Knowledge	Find a passage from TKAM Chapter 15 & 16 that addresses the herd/mob mentality and people acting like wild animals. What is Harper Lee trying to communicate in the passage?
2	Comprehension	Explain what Judge Taylor means in this quote: *"There has been a request, that this courtroom be cleared of spectators, or at least of women and children, a request that will be denied for the time being.* **People generally see what they look for and hear what they listen for,** *and they have the right to subject their children to it, but I can assure you of one thing: you will receive what you see and hear in silence in this courtroom."*
3	Application	**Similes and Metaphors** are comparisons used to create an image that helps readers see and understand things in new ways. In Chapters 16-17, Lee compares Judge Taylor, Bob Ewell, and Mayella Ewell to certain animals. Record the character and write the animal to which it was compared and discuss what Lee is saying about the character's personality by using this comparison.
4	Analysis	Dissect Mr. Ewell's testimony (pages 227-238). As the reader, what assumptions/conclusions about Mr. Ewell can we make from his words/ actions. Create a table in which you record 3 of Mr. Ewell's words/ actions and make an assumption about his life or personality based on each example.
5	Synthesis	Read the bottom of page 170. What about the Ewell's yard surprises the citizens of Maycomb? Why is this so shocking? What do you think the flowers symbolize?
6	Evaluation	Reread Scout's description of the Ewell family on page 170. Decide if you agree or disagree with Scout. What, if anything, should be done about families like the Ewells? Do the citizens of Maycomb have an obligation to support people like the Ewells?

FIGURE 4.1B Or, students can work at a more challenging pace.

INVITATION TO ENRICHMENT

Meeting advanced learners' needs can happen during all stages of learning, not just as a summative assessment. Sturtevant (2017) described an enrichment experience that an eighth-grade teacher created using a separate Google Classroom inside her traditional classroom. Based on grades, work ethic, and creativity, select students were given a special invitation and code to participate in this virtual classroom where they could find enrichment work. Students were so intrigued by the special Google Classroom that it raised the level of work *all* the students did in order to be part of this elusive learning experience. In your own class, you can decide what the requirements and characteristics are for participating students so that no one feels left out. You can use a virtual classroom like this as a select club or gifted program that can offer a compacted curriculum, accelerated curriculum, and enrichment opportunities. When given a challenge, most students rise to the occasion.

JIGSAWS AND THE TIMES

Advanced readers are looking for challenging texts to read. Whether literary or nonfictional, choice reading in the classroom allows all students to find their "just right text." Many of the reading units in my classroom offer three or more book selections to support a wide variety of readers. Students sample the books, and then choose the one that they want to read.

Choice is beneficial with shorter texts as well, and jigsaw activities enable you to provide a range of four or more texts at various reading levels all centered on a particular theme or topic. A cooperative learning activity, a jigsaw allows students to read a specific text, share their insight and findings with a small group, and then collaborate with other students to synthesize and evaluate all the readings into a whole. Advanced readers might receive a more complex text to work with than their ELL classmates, because the passages can be at multiple reading levels. When the individual readers subsequently join together in small groups, like putting together a puzzle to build a picture, they can construct a greater understanding that includes all the readings.

FIGURE 4.2 is an example of a jigsaw to introduce background information about the short story writer William Sydney Porter whose pen name was O. Henry. For this particular jigsaw, I provided three biographies about O. Henry, each catering to a distinct reading level. The articles are color-coded and every student receives the same cover sheet with directions so as not to call attention to the different readings each student is presented with. Students read the article closely, taking notes in the margins and underlining important details. Then, I sort the students into small groups (one of each article per group) to answer a series of questions that requires all three articles to answer. Students work cooperatively to pull together the information from the various articles and make connections between the author and the characters in his short stories. The complexity of the texts range to support the diverse readers in the class. Jigsaws come in all shapes and sizes and can be modified to support the students in your classroom by text and activities.

Who Was William Sydney Porter?

If his life were a short story, who'd ever believe it? -- Bruce Watson

Directions: You will read a non-fiction biography about O. Henry's life. Remember to employ the elements of nonfiction in order to fully comprehend the text.

You will:

- Actively Read the article

Annotations you might use while reading:

- *Underline important information*
- *? next to confusing information*
- *! next to shocking or surprising information*
- *Circle around unfamiliar vocabulary words*
- *Notes in the margin about what you have read*

- When you are finished, you will get together with two people who have read different articles. Put your information together to complete the O. Henry Scavenger Hunt questions. You will need information from all three articles.

- Answer the synthesis questions on the back of the scavenger hunt together as a group.

FIGURE 4.2
In this jigsaw activity, students read different biographies about the author O. Henry and then collaborate to complete a scavenger hunt about his life and its impact on his writing.

Scan the QR Code to Access the Scavenger Hunt

O. Henry Article 1

O. Henry Article 2

O. Henry Article 3

Putting together a jigsaw requires teachers to be resourceful and find different texts around a similar theme or topic. *The New York Times* Learning Network offers links to resources available on *The New York Times'* website to help you build lessons and address topics relevant to current events and literacy (**TABLE 4.1**). The "Text to Text" lesson plans pair young adult texts with current events articles from *The New York Times* and can help you pair text

TABLE 4.1   FIVE RESOURCES USING *THE NEW YORK TIMES*

THE LEARNING NETWORK offers lesson plan ideas, cross-curricular ideas, writing prompts, and contests for students. This is worth following as a blog and on Twitter for the abundance of resources and ideas that fill the site. Also, at "Any Day's Times" you can find handouts and activities to use with any print copy of *The New York Times*.

TIMES WIRE offers news directly from the journalists themselves with links to news as it happens. The Times Wire continuously updates the latest news and stories are posted as soon as they happen, 24 hours a day.

TIMES TOPICS is sort of like *The New York Times'* own Wikipedia page. Choose a topic, and you will find a summary, related articles from the newspaper, additional web resources, and digital archives from as far back at 1851. If you do a Times Topic search on Mars, for example, among the results is an article from *The New York Times* from 1924.

TIMES VIDEO is a page of *The New York Times'* own videos directly from the newsroom, presented by its journalists. There are so many great resources here alone to use with your students.

NYT VR is an app that offers a library of 360-degree virtual reality experiences. The page offers multiple collections of virtual-reality films, including "The Daily 360," which features a new 360-degree video from somewhere in the world each day. (For more ideas on how you can use NYT VR, see Chapter 3.)

for jigsaws. The September 21, 2017 "Text to Text" lesson plan, for instance, paired stories about individuals with disabilities with R.J. Palacio's novel *Wonder* (2012). There are more than thirty text pairing lesson plans on The Learning Network with classic and contemporary texts. Additionally, the website offers writing and discussion prompts. As Knowledge Constructors, teachers, as well as students, "curate information from digital resources and methods to create collections of artifacts that demonstrate meaningful connections or conclusions" (ISTE, 2016). We, therefore, need to be collectors and curators building a repertoire of texts that support learning objectives and address curriculum topics.

BLOGS, VLOGS, AND AURAS: WRITING ABOUT READING

The majority of the time that students are reading, a teacher-created assignment isn't far behind. Beyond the ordinary short responses or essay, you can offer more creative assignments, such as blogs, vlogs, and auras, for students to share their evaluation and synthesis of a text.

Classroom book blogs enable students to share book reviews about the books they read with a larger audience beyond the classroom walls. Google Schools, those using Google Classroom and other Google programs, can use Google's blogging website, Blogger, to create their own blog or to set up a classroom blog. Students can also share book reviews on Goodreads or Amazon, but creating a classroom blog builds community. Depending on the age of the students, you can put them in charge of administering the daily or weekly blog posts. You could also create a board of reviewers, students who are interested in reviewing blog submissions by other students and keeping the blog current. Putting students in charge of the blog gives students ownership and promotes student voice.

Building on the book blog and in addition to writing book reviews for the classroom blog, using HP Reveal (formerly Aurasma) can make the reviews

BLOG POST ENTRY FORMAT CHOICES

On your classroom book blog, students can get creative by writing book reviews, sharing book trailers, or creating digital book flyers to promote reading. For example, my students have the choice of four formats to post:

- **BOOK TALK FLYER.** Create a one-page document that briefly describes, summarizes, and sells the books to your classmates. Your flyers must include key information about the book, who might be interested in reading it, key review quotes that you find or create that suggest the importance of the book, and why your peers might find it interesting. Your flyer must also include visuals: a picture of the cover of the book and any other images that you think might help draw a reader into the book.

- **BOOK TRAILER.** Create an original video presentation designed to motivate others to check out the book. Just like a preview of an upcoming movie, a book trailer is a short video that previews the text. The preview can use live-action movie making, animation, or a mashup of images using sound, dialogue, and music to entice viewers to read the book. (For examples of students' trailers, see the YouTube playlist at goo.gl/H6BHqG or scan the QR code.)

- **TOP TEN POST.** Create a list of ten related titles that share similar themes, issues, or genre. You can also think of this as "If You Like… Check Out…" recommendations. Don't just list alternative book choices, however, explain how the recommended book is similar to your book.

- **BOOK REVIEW.** Write a review of the book. Book reviews contain both a summary and personal response. Feel free to create a podcast, video cast, or written review.

STUDENT BOOK TRAILERS

stand out. HP Reveal is an augmented reality app that enables teachers and students to attach an *overlay* video, animation, or image to a *trigger* image. Initially, you see the trigger image. When you scan the trigger with the HP Reveal app on a smartphone or tablet, the video, animation, or image appears and plays. Together the trigger and overlay assembly are called an *aura* (**FIGURE 4.3**). Both you and your students can create auras and use HP Reveal for enrichment opportunities. You could create auras for interactive word walls, book reviews, and for scaffolding information for diverse students learners. Students create auras to share reading and writing.

FIGURE 4.3
Scan the book cover, the trigger image for this aura (left), to see the book review (right).

In my classroom, I devote a bulletin board to showcase aura book reviews. After a student reads a book for reading workshop, I have the student record a video book review, or vlog (a video blog post, rather than a written blog post), showcasing the book and reviewing it for the class. Vlogs include a summary of the story and the student's reactions to it. Students use an image of the book cover to create the aura's trigger that displays in the classroom. These technology tools allow students to be creative with digital tools, share their knowledge with others, and build reading, writing, and speaking skills.

HYPERDOCS TO GUIDE STUDENT READING

HyperDocs are digital documents, similar to a Google Docs document, where all aspects of learning are pulled together in one place. Within the document, students are provided with hyperlinks to all aspects of the inquiry unit—videos, slideshows, images, and activities—for the student to complete and gain understanding. Students have multi-modal opportunities for learning, and there is less teacher lecturing at the front of the class. Jennifer Gonzalez, blogger and editor-in-chief of *Cult of Pedagogy* described the advantages of a playlist-style HyperDoc as follows:

> With playlists, the responsibility for executing the learning plan shifts: Students are given the unit plan, including access to all the lessons (in text or video form), ahead of time. With the learning plan in hand, students work through the lessons and assignments at their own pace. And because each student has her own digital copy of the [HyperDoc] playlist (delivered through a system like Google Classroom), the teacher can customize the list to meet each student's needs. (2016)

HyperDocs allow students to work at their own pace and offer a "road map" for student learning. Depending on the HyperDoc the teacher makes, differentiated activities and technology-rich assignments can help students learn and show their understanding while completing the activities included on the HyperDoc. Teachers might have students complete only a certain number activities on the HyperDoc or require students to complete them all; this is personal preference. Either way, by designing HyperDocs for students, teachers fulfill the Designer and Facilitator Standards for Educators (ISTE, 2017).

FIGURE 4.4 shows a HyperDoc I created for a Holocaust and WWII book club unit, which integrated English and social studies. As you can see, the HyperDoc includes individual student assignments and collaborative activities for students to discuss their reading with their peers. For this unit, students select one of the titles to read in their book club groups, and book club members meet weekly over the course of the unit. Book clubs are excellent opportunities for student-centered and student-driven learning. Within literature circles or book clubs, students determine the group roles and a reading schedule, taking ownership of the reading inquiry. Based on the students in your class, you can decide to have students meet for book club twice a week for about twenty minutes per session or designate an entire period for book clubs to meet. Additionally, you could have students screencast, voice record, or video their book discussions and post highlights to share.

WWII HYPERDOC

World War II & Holocaust Book Clubs

Keep Memory Alive

Read through Elie Wiesel's Nobel Peace Prize acceptance speech. Towards the end of his speech he states, "Neutrality helps the oppressor, never the victim. Silence encourages the tormentor, never the tormented.". *How does your book support or negate this statement? In an extended response use textual evidence to support your claim.*

Book Club Meeting #1

Meet with your literature circles/book club members to discuss the reading and your reactions. What questions, predictions, and insight. Add your discussion highlights to the Literature Circles Slide Deck.

Book Club Meeting #3

Meet with your literature circles/book club members to discuss the reading and your reactions. What questions, predictions, and insight. Add your discussion highlights to the Literature Circles Slide Deck.

Character Development

Who is the protagonist and how does the war impact their life and actions? Are they an upstander, bystander, ally, or target? Create a character web on Sketchboard detailing your character's development.

Best Quote

Add your quotes to the Google Slides or to write and illustrate one of your favourite quotes from the book. Be sure to include the book title, why you picked this quote.

Tracking the Central Idea
Use Google Slides or Prezi to map out the central idea in the text pulling textual evidence to support the claim. Be sure to include an explanation with each textual detail to articulate your thinking and reasoning.

Book Club Meeting #2

Meet with your literature circles/book club members to discuss the reading and your reactions. What questions, predictions, and insight. Add your discussion highlights to the Literature Circles Slide Deck.

Learn About the Author

Learn about the author and his/her ideas about the book and the actual events). Create a biographical infographic or presentation about the author.

The Teaching Factor™ 2017
@teachingfactor

FIGURE 4.4
HyperDocs can include individual assignments, collaborative ones, or both, like this one created for an eighth-grade small-group book club. The HyperDoc helped students monitor their reading and understanding of the books.

Technology allows students to take a leadership role in their learning and in the classroom. HyperDocs, book clubs, and literature circles enable students take the lead in the classroom as facilitators of their reading discussions, and this in turn, builds communication and collaboration skills. The ISTE Standards for Students specify that students "communicate information and ideas effectively to multiple audiences using a variety of media and formats" (ISTE, 2016). This is what we want for our students: for them to be independent, to articulate how they learn best, and to initiate and take ownership in their own education.

BLENDING BOOKS AND SOCIAL MEDIA TO PROMOTE READING: TWITTER BOOK CLUBS

Books are meant to be shared and discussed with others like a delicious meal or a fabulous new find. Many students and teachers alike already share thoughts on social media, so why not expand on this idea and try microblogging to encourage the voracious readers in your class to share thoughts about great books? By organizing a Twitter book club you can leverage social media as a tool for learning to increase student motivation and engagement about books, while at the same time modeling the use of technology as a means for learning and digital citizenship. A powerful social media tool that allows people to engage in conversations and discuss topics that are relevant to their lives, Twitter also can be an alternative space and virtual book club for students to discuss new, interesting, and noteworthy texts beyond the classroom walls. Over the years since I began using Twitter for book clubs, they have grown from a project for my classroom's avid readers into an anticipated monthly discussion among the majority of students.

SETTING UP A TWITTER BOOK CLUB

Organizing a Twitter book club is relatively simple. As with any book club, you'll need to choose books, set a reading schedule, and specify dates for discussions. The difference is with a Twitter book club, those discussions will take place online in a chat via Twitter with students typing tweets to share their opinions, insights, and questions. Every student will need a Twitter account and handle (an online name that begins with the @ symbol) to participate and need to include the book club's designated hashtag in their tweets. Even if you and some of your students already have personal accounts, I recommend creating separate, dedicated accounts for educational purposes—with classroom-appropriate handles.

The week before your first Twitter book club chat, make sure students are all aware of not only how to use Twitter, but also how you expect them to use it. In class, give each student a cheat sheet that covers the "dos and don'ts" of tweeting, explains the anatomy of a tweet, and outlines your class rules for a Twitter book club chat. I also hold meetings and tutorial sessions after school to introduce Twitter and offer a "how-to" demonstration of setting up a Twitter account and using Twitter.

To be part of a specific conversation on Twitter, such as the book club chat, all the tweets must include the same hashtag (an identifying phrase). Before your first Twitter book club chat, designate a specific hashtag for students to follow the conversation and contribute to the book chat. For example, I use the hashtag #RMS8R: the Twitter-required # sign, followed by the initials of our school (RMS), the student grade level (8), and the team (R). I use the same hashtag for each new book and Twitter chat for consistency and so as not to confuse students by changing up the hashtags each month.

PERMISSIONS AND CONDUCT

To ease potential parental concerns about using social media in the classroom, clearly communicate your intentions for your Twitter book club at its outset. At the beginning of the school year when I first introduce the project to students, for example, I present a "Twitter Permission Letter and Code of Conduct" (**FIGURE 4.5**) for students to take home to their parents and guardians.

Your permission letter should address your intentions and objectives for using Twitter for the book club assignment and stress the importance of practicing digital citizenship. To confirm that parents or guardians receive and read your letter, require them and their students to sign it and return it prior to the first Twitter book club chat. Students should not be allowed to participate until you have received the signed letter of consent.

FIGURE 4.5 Before students can participate in the Twitter book chat, make sure they have returned a signed "Parent Permission Letter and Twitter Code of Conduct" like this one. ➤

Dear Parents and Guardians,

Throughout the school year, English 8R students are encouraged to read to learn about their world, strengthen their reading abilities, and enjoy great books. Each month, students are invited to participate in a book club where we use Twitter as a discussion platform to collaborate and converse with our peers about the books we are reading. This letter is to give you more information about the project and to address internet safety.

As you know, Twitter is a micro-blogging tool that is designed to allow acquaintances to stay in touch with each other, report the news, engage in a conversation, or share information. For this project, I would like students to create a Twitter account that they would use for school purposes only. Each month, students will access Twitter to participate in a Twitter chat. They will answer and raise questions about topics addressed in the books by using the hashtag #RMS8R.

Students will understand that they can partake in social media for educational purposes, and they will learn to practice positive digital citizenship behavior. By signing this contract students understand that they will continue to uphold the school's Internet Acceptable Use Policy and engage in the book chats only for the purpose intended.

On Twitter, a tweet can be a maximum of 280 characters, including spaces and punctuation. Students include the book club hashtag with their tweet so that everyone who is part of the conversation can view the tweets (**FIGURE 4.6**), as opposed to just the tweets of people they are following. Following everyone in a Twitter book club is not necessary, because the hashtag alone allows students to view all the tweets presented during the Twitter chat. Students also include specific handles in their tweets to directly address a person who said or asked something in a prior tweet. (To see Twitter book chats in action, join the conversations mentioned in the "Capture Their Interest: Offering Book Choice" section of Chapter 1.)

FIGURE 4.6
Twitter book club discussions can be collaborative, such as this chat about Leland Melvin's *Chasing Space* (2017) among eighth-grade students, myself, and our school's Earth science teacher.

STUDENT VOICE

During the Twitter book club chats students share their own stories, make connections, and critically address the issues in the text. Shy and quiet students who have insightful responses but are not comfortable sharing in front of the whole class are often less intimidated posting on Twitter. Everyone has a voice, and if a student is not tweeting then he or she is not part of the dialogue. The idea to stress is that each student has to be part of the conversation because all voices and tweets matter.

To help get the conversation started, you can certainly post questions during the Twitter book chat, but once students are talking with each other in the online environment, give them space to support and respond to each other's ideas. Enable students to lead the discussion, post questions, make connections, share reactions, and maybe even start side conversations about their reading, the characters, or the book's setting. Often, students who might not talk to each other face-to-face in class, don't hesitate to respond to each other online, offer constructive suggestions, and piggy-back on each other's ideas. Students in my class rapidly learned that a retweet pointing out an insightful comment was like a high-five, and they looked forward to teacher- and peer-retweets of their comments in agreement or support. Coordinating with your colleagues, you can change the dynamics of interactions to include students from multiple classes in your Twitter book club chat, so your students can discuss with friends and peers beyond their classmates. When students hear from a larger audience, they can learn new things and hear different perspectives that influence and reinforce their thinking.

BEST BOOKS FOR TWEETING

A perennial question for any book club is how to choose the books students read. In my classroom, books are voted on, but I try to keep half the titles related to concurrent classroom content and the other half new and noteworthy young adult titles. For example, during our dystopian unit, students first voted whether to read George Orwell's *Animal Farm* (1990), Lois Lowry's *The Giver*, or Neal Shusterman's *Unwind* (2009) for class. At the same time, the selected Twitter book club book was Candace Fleming's *The Family Romanov: Murder, Rebellion, and the Fall of Imperial Russia* (2014) about the Russian Revolution. With its direct historical connections, *The Family Romanov* was a perfect pairing to help students to understand the historical context in *Animal Farm*, while at the same time it resonated with other dystopian society themes. Pairing English and social studies texts also shows students the interconnectedness of the two disciplines and brings additional insight to their understanding of history. Likewise, Victoria Aveyard's *Red Queen* (2015) and its sequel *Glass Sword* (2016) are two contemporary dystopian novels that would pair well.

TWEETING WITH AUTHORS

Social media can bring teachers and students closer to amazing writers and thinkers: Many authors are on Twitter and are happy to discuss their books with students. Search for an author's name, then follow his or her account, and then tweet the author a message. I usually try to be brief but specific, such as,

> *My 8th grade students and I are reading and discussing your book* [title]. *Would you be available on* [date] *at* [time] *for 15 minutes to join the chat and answer student questions about your book?*

Some authors are easy to access and happy to participate. Even if an author has a schedule conflict or otherwise can't attend, I often still include the author's handle in the tweets during the chat so he or she can follow along, like, or respond at a later time.

Tweeting with authors allows readers to ask questions for a deeper understanding of the text. For example, award-winning author Jason Reynolds agreed to participate in a Twitter book club chat with my students about his book *All American Boys* (2015), which he cowrote with Brendan Kiely. Set in the present day, the powerful story centers on the effects of racial stereotyping and pairs well with *To Kill a Mockingbird*. Reading these two books side by side helped my students draw larger connections and tackle difficult conversations about race, stereotypes, and standing up for what is right. Talking/tweeting with authors in critical and reflective ways not only makes students feel inspired and important, but also gives them a glimpse into the world of professional writers and their writing processes.

BOOK CLUB BENEFITS

Our mission as teachers is to ban the boring and to use present tools to engage students, raise rigor, and help young people negotiate this world of text in all its diverse forms. Twitter is one digital media tool that can be used effectively for discussing stories and the powerful impact they have on our lives. Twitter also allows space for students to critically discuss topics that are relevant to their lives and share stories, images, and other links to meaningful texts that address the same topics. Twitter book clubs can extend discussions outside the classroom and help students to deepen their thinking through tweeting about reading. With technology, students take the lead in the conversations and are eager to read and communicate more. As my Twitter book chat participants remarked, "the book clubs pushed me to read outside of my comfort zone and enjoy new books" and "this chat allowed me to think of the reading in new ways." This is exactly what we want for our students: to read diverse texts, talk about them, and grow their reading life.

AS YOU GO FORWARD

Advanced readers want to grow their understanding and skills, not just fill their time in the classroom. Through differentiated assignments, jigsaw activities, and HyperDocs, advanced readers can challenge themselves, while other students work at their own levels too. Enrichment activities, such as Twitter book chats and invitation-only Google Classrooms, can motivate and entice all students to rise to the rigor presented through these diverse digital activities.

TABLE 4.2   PAIRING TOOLS WITH TEACHING STRATEGIES

TEACHING STRATEGY (PEDAGOGY)	TECHNOLOGY TOOLS	LINKS
Supporting advanced readers with tiered assignments and jigsaws	Google Classroom	classroom.google.com
	Jigsaw Classroom	jigsaw.org
	The New York Times Learning Network	nytimes.com/section/learning
Sharing books	Blogger	Blogger.com
Writing about books	Goodreads	goodreads.com
Personalized reading	HP Reveal	hpreveal.com
	HyperDocs	hyperdocs.co
Building critical thinking through student-directed book discussions and chats	Twitter	twitter.com

COMMON CORE STATE STANDARDS	ISTE STANDARDS FOR STUDENTS AND FOR EDUCATORS
CCSS.ELA-Literacy.CCRA.SL.2 Integrate and evaluate information presented in diverse media and formats, including visually, quantitatively, and orally.	(E) 3a. Citizen Create experiences for learners to make positive, socially responsible contributions and exhibit empathetic behavior online that build relationships and community.
CCSS.ELA-Literacy.CCRA.SL.5 Make strategic use of digital media and visual displays of data to express information and enhance understanding of presentations.	(E) 3b. Citizen Establish a learning culture that promotes curiosity and critical examination of online resources and fosters digital literacy and media fluency.
CCSS.ELA-Literacy.CCRA.SL.1 Prepare for and participate effectively in a range of conversations and collaborations with diverse partners, building on others' ideas and expressing their own clearly and persuasively.	(S) 2b. Digital Citizen Students engage in positive, safe, legal and ethical behavior when using technology, including social interactions online or when using networked devices.

CHAPTER 5

TEACHING ALL OUR READERS AT THE SAME TIME

We are all part of the same story, each of us

different chapters. We may not have the power

to choose setting or plot, but we can choose

what kind of character we want to be.

—**David Arnold,** *Kids of Appetite*

The cacophony of students in our diverse classrooms benefits all student learners, because we learn from each other. If you walked into my classroom, for example, rarely would you find me lecturing about a particular text. Instead, you'd find students working independently, at learning stations, in small groups, engaged in a flipped lesson on laptops, reading books, or working in their English notebooks. As the teacher, I am the facilitator and might be conferencing with students about their Passion Projects, eavesdropping on book discussions, checking on a group's progress through an adventure-based learning experience, or answering questions about deadlines for our global collaborative project with Japan. In this final chapter, I share some of these choice-based lessons that can engage and support the diverse readers in any classroom. From flipped lessons to gamification, these activities and the technology that supports them can help you transform your classroom into a similarly dynamic place where students learn from and support each other.

FLIPPED LESSONS

To give more attention and personalized time to your students, consider flipping your writing lessons in the classroom, rather than simply reteaching a mini-lesson or making a review lesson. TeachThought (2013) defined flipped learning as when,

> students are introduced to content at home, and practice working through it at school. In this blended learning approach, face-to-face interaction is mixed with independent study via technology. Students watch pre-recorded videos at home, then come to school to do the homework armed with questions and at least some background knowledge. (2013)

For example, I post pre-recorded lessons on YouTube and import them into Google Classroom. At any time, students can access the lessons, such as *Ways to Start an Essay, Writing and Revising Your Claim,* and *Building Better Body Paragraphs* (**FIGURE 5.1**), and they can even refer back to them later, if needed. To record your lessons, you can use a tool like Screencast-O-Matic, which is a free screencasting platform that enables you to record what's happening on your computer while you narrate what you're doing or otherwise explain the lesson content. To learn more about the flipped lesson approach, I recommend Dana Johansen and Sonja Cherry-Paul's *Flip Your Writing Workshop: A Blended Learning Approach* (2016), or you can visit my YouTube channel to view some examples (tinyurl.com/drhaiken or scan the QR code).

FLIPPED LEARNING VIDEOS

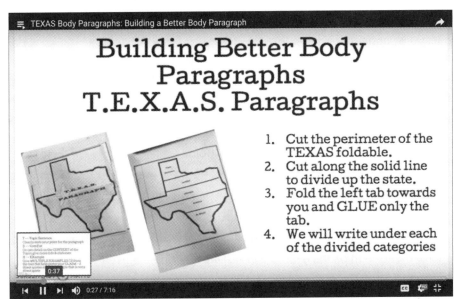

FIGURE 5.1
Using Screencast-O-Matic, I record mini-lessons students can access whenever they need a skills reminder.

DIFFERENTIATED CHOICE MENUS TO PROMOTE READING, THINKING, AND UNDERSTANDING

Differentiation is another way to provide students with individualized learning, specifically to provide choices or options based on their readiness, interests, and learning preferences (think multiple intelligences). As Carol Ann Tomlinson (2017) explained, differentiation is a way of "tailoring instruction to meet individual needs. Differentiation can be based on content, process, products, or the learning environment." Through differentiation and choice, you can provide alternative ways to help students learn and show what they know. Choice menu boards are a great way to do this, and once again technology can help. You can create choice activities for before, during, and after reading to highlight reading strategies, content understanding, and multiple intelligences. The sections that follow detail several examples of choice activities—2-5-8 choice menus, Think-Tac-Toe, Bingo boards, and task cards—that I created for use with my eighth-grade students. As you'll see, the choice menus tap into a variety of learning styles, levels of questions, and technology tools.

2-5-8 CHOICE MENU

A 2-5-8 choice menu offers nine or more activity choices, each of which is assigned 2, 5, or 8 points. The higher the point value, the more challenging the project. Students choose two activities from the menu that total 10 points. Students can complete one easy and one more challenging project or two medium projects to equal the required 10 points. Differentiated by process and product, the projects represent a variety of learning preferences. A 2-5-8 choice menu such as the example in **FIGURE 5.2** could be used after students finish reading their independent choice books, for instance. Using a variety of technology tools, the projects enable students to showcase their learning, understanding, and evaluation of the text.

THINK-TAC-TOE

A Think-Tac-Toe is a differentiation tool that offers activities that students can choose to demonstrate their understanding. Designed to be completed while or after students read a text, this choice menu is presented in the form of a tic-tac-toe board, a nine-square grid. Students are required to complete any three assignments as long as they make a three-in-row win

2 **POINTS**	▪ Write a Book Review for **AMAZON.COM** and/or **GOODREADS.COM** and add details about your reading and understanding. Be sure to rate the book. Send a copy of the link to your teacher. ▪ Create a Found Poem or Blackout Poem on **GOOGLE DOCS** about one of the themes presented in the text. Share the document with your teacher.
5 **POINTS**	▪ Create a **PODCAST** in which you are the host interviewing a main character from your book or your book's author. Develop the questions you will ask and the character's answers. If you are interviewing the author, research his or her actual responses to similar questions. Record the interview as an audio file to share on Google Classroom. ▪ Make a comic highlighting an important scene from the book using **TOONDOO OR POWTOON**. Put the pictures together using **ANIMOTO** or another movie creation tool to share on Google Classroom. ▪ Create a **GLOGSTER** glog about your book. Include the following in your glog: Title, author, image of the book, setting, characters, problem/conflict, how the problem/conflict was solved, what you liked about the book, and how you would rate the book.
8 **POINTS**	▪ Create a **TED TALK** or **VLOG** in which you address why the book you read matters today. ▪ Create a **LIVEBINDERS** binder of 10 to 15 resources for teachers who might want to use this book in their classroom. Include the author's webpage, offer teaching ideas, create a quiz or test, add videos, and more.

FIGURE 5.2 In a 2-5-8 choice menu, such as this eighth-grade summative assessment for independent reading, students may choose any two options that total 10 points.

(vertical, diagonal, or horizontal). The center of the board is a "free choice;" students can pick any project with which they can spotlight their abilities and strengths. Projects can be geared toward Gardner's Multiple Intelligences and Bloom's Taxonomy for a variety of products and to show different levels of understanding from evaluation to basic understanding. After my class finished reading Harper Lee's *To Kill a Mockingbird*, for example, I assigned the Think-Tac-Toe shown in **FIGURE 5.3**. Think-Tac-Toes can be used at any part of a reading, to access background knowledge, as an anticipation guide, for text-dependent questions during reading, as a check for understanding after reading, or as a summative assessment tool.

Choose 12 or more telling quotes and create a **THINGLINK** showcasing the quotes and elaborating on their significance.	Shoot and edit a short digital **iMOVIE** that illustrates a scene from the novel or one of the themes of the novel.	Create a 20-question multiple-choice test with an answer key on **KAHOOT!**.
Write a **BLOG POST** discussing how and why TKAM is still relevant today (500 words maximum).	***To Kill A Mockingbird*** **THINK-TAC-TOE** FREE CHOICE	Create 5 **#BOOKSNAPS** highlighting poignant scenes in the text. Use Bitmoji, Snapchat, and Google Drawings to highlight the 6 Notice & Note signposts that appear in TKAM.
Produce a book trailer for the novel using **iMOVIE** or **MOVIE MAKER**.	Create a **SCREENCAST** detailing Scout's growth throughout the text. How does she change throughout the novel? What does she learn? How does it impact her life and those around her? Which passages show "Aha Moments" of Scout's character?	Using **PREZI**, create a timeline of events for TKAM. Be sure to include images and text to illustrate the key events throughout the novel.

FIGURE 5.3 Students complete three assignments in a row on a Think-Tac-Toe board, such as this summative assessment for use after reading *To Kill a Mockingbird*.

BINGO BOARDS

Bingo boards are similar to Think-Tac-Toe boards; students choose to complete activities or projects from each column on the board to spell *bingo,* or they complete all the questions on the board. You can use Bingo boards in several ways to promote student choice and voice. For example, you can fill an entire Bingo board with text-dependent questions and instruct students to complete one row or column of the Bingo board each night as a homework assignment for the week. Or, you could use the board of questions as a formative assessment. For an in-class activity, give students a Bingo board with situations, characters, or actions and instruct students to find specific textual details or direct quotes that highlight each situation in the assigned book (**FIGURE 5.4**). Using a Bingo board as a scavenger hunt gives students a mission to uncover key events and show their understanding while reading the text in class.

| Midsummer Night's Dream Act 3				
B	**I**	**N**	**G**	**O**
Demetrius expressing his love for Helena	Hermia says something hateful to Demetrius	A metaphor becomes the literal	Bottom shows his egotism	Titania blinded by love
Helena furious	Mischievous Puck	FREE SPACE	Girl Fight	Fantasy & Reality Merge
Inept Actors	Hermia is dumped	Someone Falls Asleep	Oberon Makes Amends	Mortals acting like fools
A Serpent	Why "poor females mad"	Elements of Pyramus & Thisbe are changed	The Moon	Lysander expressing his hatred for Hermia

FIGURE 5.4 I use this Bingo board as an in-class activity for Shakespeare's *A Midsummer Night's Dream*.

BLOOM'S TAXONOMY

Bingo boards are fun, interactive, simple to make, and easy to adapt for any content area or grade level. Depending on the task created for students, the questions can tap into Bloom's Taxonomy of Questioning, encourage critical thinking, and enable you to assess student understanding. Technology integrationist, staff developer, and coauthor of *The HyperDoc Handbook* (2016), Lisa Highfill created a three-by-three Show What You Know Bingo choice menu (**FIGURE 5.5**) of iPad apps for students to show their learning and share with others. Depending on the grade level of students or complexity of the tasks, Bingo boards can have twenty-five squares or fewer.

FIGURE 5.5
Lisa Highfill, coauthor of *The HyperDoc Handbook*, created this Show What You Know Bingo to enable students to demonstrate knowledge of various iPad apps.

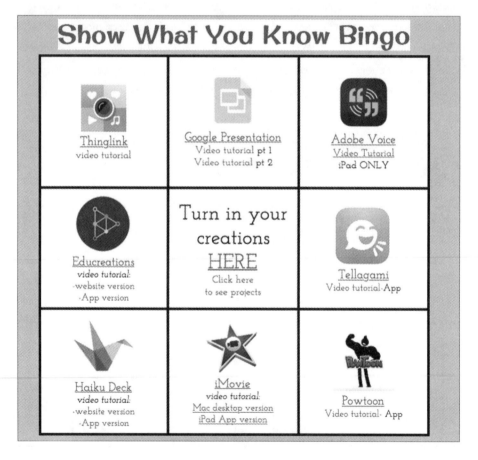

TASK CARDS

Targeting specific skills, standards, or subject areas, task cards are a set of cards with questions and activities on them that you can use for reinforcement of teaching concepts, assessment, and differentiated learning activities. Task cards can focus on Bloom's Taxonomy of Questioning and tap into multiple intelligences. For example, I designed the card set shown in **FIGURE 5.6** so that each card was specific to a layer of close reading. The cards' tasks address what the text says, means, and does. This requires students to reread parts of a text multiple times with a different lens to hone their close reading skills.

Task cards can be completed individually, in small groups, for homework, in learning centers, and even in game-like activities. Students can write their responses to the task cards and compare answers. Task cards can be used in a Beat the Clock game, seeing who can answer the task the quickest. You can also use them as checks for understanding in the middle of a lesson to see if students have digested the material.

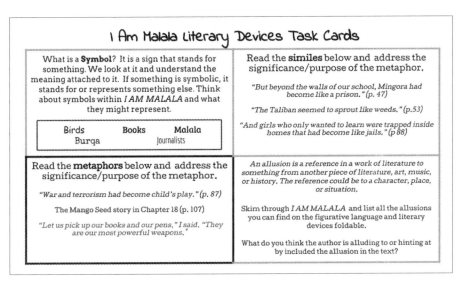

FIGURE 5.6
These task cards for a close reading of *I Am Malala* (Yousafzai, 2013) are specific to the author's craft and style.

CHOICE FOR ALL

Choice menus can be used with all students, from struggling to advanced readers. You can create choice menus based on student readiness, interests, and learning profiles. Choice in the classroom empowers students, while at the same time adheres to learning goals. When students are able to select choices that most appeal to them and that they are comfortable completing, they can master the activity and then move on to more challenging activities. When planning a choice menu, first focus on the learning outcomes before thinking about different tasks. Different choice menus can be created based on Bloom's Taxonomy of Questioning, Costa's Levels of Questioning, Gardner's Multiple Intelligences, or the ISTE Standards for Students. Choice menus allow all the diverse students in a classroom to be Empowered Learners, Knowledge Constructors, and Creative Communicators (ISTE, 2016).

INQUIRY-BASED LEARNING: PASSION PROJECTS AND GENIUS HOUR

If everything is Googleable, what is the purpose of school today? This sentiment is shared by many—reluctant and advanced readers alike. In today's digital age, students can search the internet to learn and teach themselves about anything. As a result, we teachers have had to revise our role in the classroom from all-knowledgeable lecturers to facilitators and coaches who promote critical thinking, deep reading, and effective communication skills so students are ready for college, careers, and whatever the future may bring.

To embrace these new roles for educators, teachers across the globe are tapping into the power of Genius Hour and Passion Projects. These interrelated concepts stem from Google's 20% rule for its employees. Google Innovator, Jeff Heil explained, "Google has a policy of allowing its employees to dedicate 20 percent of their time to personal projects that they hope will eventually equate to new products/services. The idea is that if you allow your employees to follow their passions, good things will happen" (2017). Daniel H. Pink, author of *Drive: The Surprising Truth About What Motivates Us* (2011), also suggested that "sixty minutes a week of noncommissioned work can electrify your job" (2011). Good things do result: Gmail was sparked from Google's 20% rule.

This business trend has spilled over into the classroom with the idea that if students have a set amount of time each week to work on a project they are interested in, a Passion Project, students will be more creative and become lifelong learners. Angela Maiers and Amy Sandvold first wrote about "Genius Hour" in their book *The Passion-Driven Classroom: A Framework for Teaching and Learning* (2010). Maiers has gone on to promote genius in everyone and illustrate passion-driven learning as a classroom essential. In her book *Liberating Genius*, she stated, "Genius Hour is a nearly unprecedent-ed opportunity for teachers to guide students in how to be effective learners and citizens, by helping them connect what they do in school to the broader community. It's our job to nurture our geniuses so they can change the world" (2016, p. 15).

Genius Hour provides students a choice in what they learn because the Passion Projects they work on are self-selected. Genius Hour is not so much about an end product, but really about the process of research, exploration, failure, and grit. During Genius Hour the object is that students tinker with ideas, test, create, master, and build. For example, every Friday in my class-room, students spend a Genius Hour working on a Passion Project that has one or more of the learning outcomes:

✦ Help make the world a better place.

✦ Research a question that can't be answered with a Google search.

✦ Create or make something.

✦ Learn or master a new skill.

Each semester students choose a project to work on during Genius Hour and then, when it's complete, to share with the class, the school, the community, and the world. Passion Projects allow students to explore their talents, cultivate their interests, and build necessary skills beyond those that the Common Core State Standards define as college and career readiness skills.

ENCOURAGING GENIUS IN THE CLASSROOM

To help students tap into interests and abilities beyond what traditional school measures, begin by brainstorming and defining "genius," as well as what a genius looks and acts like. Sharing other examples and definitions of genius can stimulate discussion. For instance, Seth Godin offered a multifaceted illustration of genius,

A genius solves a problem in a way no one else could.

A genius looks at a problem with fresh eyes.

A genius changes the rules.

A genius is someone who's willing to do the work of a human being.

A genius is ready make a unique impact on the world; solve a problem in a new way.

A genius gives the world something it didn't know was missing. (as cited in Maiers, 2011, p. ix)

To encourage students to look for genius in themselves, I ask students to complete a Genius Inventory on Google Forms that asks the questions:

✦ What matters to you most?

✦ What are you an expert in?

✦ What subject area are you most excited to learn about?

✦ What do you like doing in your spare time?

✦ If you could take a class on anything, what would it be?

✦ What does "genius" mean to you?

Student responses can be merged in a word cloud using Tagxedo and shared for further discussion (**FIGURE 5.7**).

FIGURE 5.7 Use the Tagxedo website to create a word cloud after your classroom brainstorm of "What is genius?"

Additionally, encourage students to look for models of their defined aspects of genius in your community and globally. Share examples of people who exemplify genius and collect stories about teens who are doing genius things to highlight the amazing potential of young people, inspire your students, and show them that young people can make a difference, start a business, master a skill, and empower others. For example, entrepreneurial sixth-grader Moziah Bridges started his own bow tie company called Mo's Bows (mosbowsmemphis.com). Likewise, the stuffed toy company ShelterPups (shelterpups.com) was started because a young Theodora Verhagen wondered why no stuffed dogs looked like the mixed breed dogs her family adopted from a local animal shelter. She thought that should change, and her parents helped her bring her idea to fruition. The resulting company now sells handmade, felted dogs and cats, donating a portion of the profits to real animal shelters. For older students, you could mention Malala Yousafzai, the teenage education rights activist and Nobel Peace Prize recipient, and Jake Andraka, the teenage inventor, scientist, and cancer researcher.

Models help students see themselves in others and illustrate the power that an idea, a question, and even a prototype can be launched into a business or invention. Two of my students still serve as an inspiration for my classes: They organized both a book drive and t-shirt fundraiser for their Passion Project during Genius Hour. Because of their endeavors, nearly 1,000 books were collected, inscribed with a personal message, and sent to schools and organizations in neighboring communities that lacked resources. In addition, they designed and sold S.P.A.R.K. (Spread Passion and Reading Knowledge) t-shirts on the website Booster.com (**FIGURE 5.8**) to raise awareness and money for schools in need. As the students stated in their Passion Project reflection, "We chose this project because we believe that books are a key learning tool and also to spread our love of learning. We both value our education and the opportunities we have. We want to spread our passion for reading and learning to others. We decided the best way to 'ignite their spark' was to motivate them by giving them books." Both students were resourceful and creative in their project. Each week they planned and promoted their project to spread the word and expand their original idea to help schools in need. They came into school even after the school year had ended to continue to organize the books for delivery and hold a book-signing breakfast.

FIGURE 5.8
As part of their Passion Project, two students designed a t-shirt as a fund-raiser to buy books for schools in need.

Over the years of initiating Genius Hour and Passion Projects, I have had students who have gone on to create blogs, write movie scripts, and even teach music classes for preschoolers at the public library. Every year I am inspired by my students' Passion Projects, their dedication, and the impact it makes on others. When students have ownership in their learning, they become leaders and teachers to others. Student inquiry drives research, reading, and mastery. What amazing projects and ideas might your students come up with?

CULTIVATING PASSION PROJECTS

How do students get from the brainstorm and inspiration stage to formulating their projects? Through brain-boosting activities and questionnaires, you can help students pinpoint an idea they want to work on for an entire term (semester, trimester, or quarter, depending on the district). For example, you can have students each articulate several possible projects on a teacher-created document on Google Forms, and then research and collect information about their various topics for about two to four weeks. After they learn more about each option, they each confirm their passion commitment for the semester. When you give students the choice to research anything they want, they are not at a loss for ideas.

To help students clarify and articulate their intentions and goals for their newly chosen Passion Projects, I ask students to write one clear and concise sentence in the future tense describing the achievement of their project. My inspiration for this assignment was the success Long Island artist and art educator Tim Needles had when he asked his high school students to imagine what goals they would like to achieve in their lifetime then to write from the perspective of a future in which they'd completed those goals.

To coincide with the One Sentence assignment, I also ask students to create a "digital inspiration" to highlight their project intentions for Genius Hour. These digital inspirations become not only inspirations to the students, but also advertisements of sorts to inform others of their work (**FIGURE 5.9**). Sharing them with the whole school, I post all of my student's digital inspirations with their Passion Project sentences in the hallways to remind my students of the power of their ideas. (This idea came from Carol Varsalona's blog *Beyond LiteracyLink*; Carol collects photographs and poems from published writers and teachers, which she calls "digital inspirations.")

FIGURE 5.9
Using her own drawings to showcase her digital inspiration and Passion Project, this student used Genius Hour to study, practice, and develop her craft as an artist.

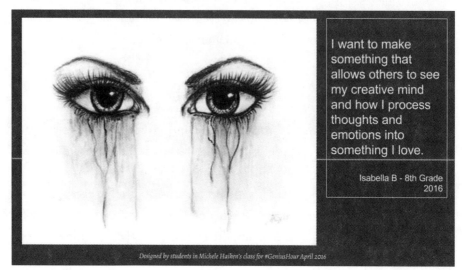

I want to make something that allows others to see my creative mind and how I process thoughts and emotions into something I love.

Isabella B - 8th Grade
2016

Designed by students in Michele Haiken's class for #GeniusHour April 2016

The One Sentence project articulates the learning outcomes the students each identify for themselves, and then sets the course for the work they are going to accomplish for the remainder of the semester.

ELEVATOR PITCH AND GENIUS HOUR SHARK TANK

The digital inspiration is just the beginning of students' projects and Genius Hour activities. After a few weeks of research, examination, creating, and making, have students create an elevator pitch about their project: a persuasive speech that lasts about the length of an elevator ride and further explains their passion and project intentions. The Elevator Pitch assignment requires students to extend their ideas in the One Sentence project and to effectively communicate their ideas to someone other than their peers and teacher. For example, I invite former students into the classroom on the day of the pitches to evaluate and give feedback to my students in a *Shark Tank*–style setting. To help students craft their pitches, you can use a graphic organizer, such as the one shown in **FIGURE 5.10**, as a writing guide.

GENIUS HOUR SHARK TANK PITCH

FIGURE 5.10
A graphic organizer can help students think through and write down what they will say during their elevator pitches.

Background & Knowledge: Clearly state the purpose of, use of, and need for your project and the problem it solves.	
Personal Passion: Why is this project so important to you? What made you interested in this project? What strengths and expertise do you bring to your own Passion Project?	
Process: What does your project entail? What are the steps you have completed and STILL have to complete for it to come to fruition?	
Results: What are you hoping to learn/gain from the Passion Project? What is the end result?	

Because the projects created in Genius Hour are projects students are passionate about, writing and talking about their ideas and outcomes is not as difficult as writing a literary essay or taking a test. My students have brought in music samples, food samples, and photos to share with peers and guest judges. The Elevator Pitch assignment gives students the opportunity to show initiative and insight, as well as present research to support their ideas.

GENIUS BLOGGING AND SNAPGUIDE

Because Genius Hour is really a process of researching, playing, making, and exploring, it is important for students to document the process as they work. The method can be a matter of student choice—a Snapguide, a blog, a podcast, or another teacher-approved option. For example, with the website and app Snapguide, students can create their own step-by-step guides showing images and descriptions for each stage of their process, similar to a WikiHow or a simplified YouTube video. To illustrate their guides and document their projects, students can take weekly pictures, highlighting the work they do during Genius Hour.

Blogs are another excellent tool for documenting Passion Projects and a great venue for students to share their Genius Hour learning with a larger global audience. One of my students created a blog in which she described her step-by-step process of each week baking a dessert from countries all around the world. She included pictures and descriptions of the process she went through selecting the recipes and then baking and blogging about her culinary adventures (**FIGURES 5.11** and **5.12**). Other students have created blogs to write about writing, share their love of books, or deconstruct episodes of the Netflix series *Stranger Things*.

FIGURE 5.11
For her Passion Project, one student baked desserts from around the world and created a blog to highlight the recipes for and results of her weekly baking.

FIGURE 5.12
The same student documented the behind-the-scenes process of her baking and blogging project in a second blog.

WAYS TO PRESENT CULMINATING PASSION PROJECTS

The processes of learning, making, and researching are all important for Genius Hour. At the same time, we teachers want students to celebrate and share their learning. Beyond traditional presentations, students can present their Passion Project learning to their peers, teacher, and community in many creative and technology-rich ways. Offer students a choice of technology projects that are "learner driven and provide alternative ways for students to demonstrate competency" (ISTE Standards for Educators, 2017). The following are a selection of project choices with which I have allowed students to share their expertise:

+ **SKETCHNOTE.** Show visually what you did for your Passion Project in by sketchnoting the process and learning during Genius Hour in a visually appealing story map.

+ **BREAKOUT EDU.** Breakout EDU is an interactive game that requires players to work together to crack codes, open locks, and solve puzzles connected by theme or topic. Complete a Breakout EDU Game Design Template Worksheet, and create a way to combine critical thinking with your Passion Project topic. You can use any of the Breakout EDU components to challenge your classmates and help them think deeply about your project.

+ **RADIOLAB-STYLE PODCAST.** *RadioLab* is a show on NPR that presents topics through engaging conversations, media clips, and investigative journalism. Create your own *RadioLab*-style podcast and share the audio file to publish a collection of Genius Hour podcasts online. Check out *RadioLab*'s website for more information and to listen to a few podcasts before you get started.

+ **VIDEO TED TALK.** TED is a group devoted to spreading ideas. Its national conferences and regional TEDx events are famous for offering short, powerful talks, which are then posted online. Present your own TED-style talk about your Passion Project topic. Video it and share it with your teacher to post on the class Genius Hour YouTube channel. The TED Talk should be informative, engaging, and inspiring. Camera shy? Present your TED Talk live in front of the class.

✦ **FEATURE ARTICLE.** Write a feature article for an online teen magazine or the school newspaper. Try to get it published (although if it isn't, your grade won't be affected). Share your genius process and final product with the world.

✦ **WHITEBOARD ANIMATION VIDEO.** Tell your story and genius process through a whiteboard animation video. Record and start drawing. Use video editing tools to speed it up to four times its normal speed and add a voiceover and music.

✦ **PREZI SCREENCAST.** Create a Prezi presentation and then screencast an audio presentation talking through the major points of your Passion Project. Offer additional information to support the images and text included in your Prezi presentation. Use a free screencasting site, such as Screencast-O-Matic, to create your screencast presentation.

Teaching and learning is a reflective process. In her book *Students Taking Charge: Inside the Learner-Active, Technology-Infused Classroom*, Nancy Sulla argued,

> It's time to think through what schooling looks like and make some significant adjustments to past practices with three critical goals for instructional design: engage students in learning, build greater responsibility for student learning, and increase academic rigor. (2011, p. 3)

Passion Projects and Genius Hour engage and empower students, because students are in charge of what they are learning about and how they will demonstrate their knowledge in the world beyond the classroom. It is through these learning opportunities that students are building skills in creativity, problem-solving, critical thinking, communication, and leadership—the tools they will need to do meaningful work that will make a positive impact on their future and the world's.

GAMIFICATION: LEARNING AS A QUEST-BASED ADVENTURE

Gamification, also called quest-based learning, is an approach to learning that connects meaningful gaming with content objectives to promote learning and deepen student understanding. Through gamification you can transform literacy instruction into a game with creativity, collaboration, and play, while still meeting Common Core State Standards and ISTE Standards for Students. Exactly how you bring games and game playing into the classroom is really a matter of thinking creatively and playfully about what you already do. For example, you could tie assignments to point values and badges, which students could then use to unlock privileges, such as a homework pass or preferential seating. As with choice menus, students would choose which assignments to complete and when, but with the aim of collecting as many points as possible or a "literacy champion" selection of badges. Alternately, you could organize an overarching mission in which assignments are like a sequence of game levels. Students would need to successfully complete each assignment in order to "rank up" to the next and eventually complete all the required material.

In my classroom, gamification has helped to engage even reluctant students, build collaboration and teamwork, and boost literacy skills. Each reading unit features a quest for students to complete during their reading of the unit's text. All year long students uncover the mysteries and powers in the books and other texts they read. Each unit features puzzles, quests, and challenges; students might earn badges for completing various tasks or collect points during an adventure quest to show what they're learning or thinking about a text. Students unlock the secrets hidden in text, go on scavenger hunts, and race through quests (think *The Amazing Race* for literacy) to show their understanding and knowledge. To differentiate learning, some students may take side quests, while others might fast-forward to the level-ending boss battles or solve mysteries that help unlock the legends, themes, and pertinent information.

DYSTOPIAN MISSIONS

One of the best ways to understand how gamification can transform a reading unit is to consider an example. In my classroom's dystopian reading unit, students select a dystopian book to read based on their interests and reading abilities, and then they complete missions to show their understanding and collect badges or experience points (XP). Students are given time in class to read, and throughout the unit, I present mini-lessons that cover specific elements of dystopian literature. The students then apply the content of these mini-lessons to the specific missions and adventures to show their understanding of the text.

I designed the Dystopian Reading Quest so that students could work independently to complete various missions and show their thinking about their reading. Students have a choice of which missions to work towards and in what order; some missions are requirements, whereas others are enrichment. Because students are looking to amass as many XP points as possible, they might aim to complete the higher scoring missions or to complete as many missions as possible. Completing a mission does not automatically equate with the earned points, however; quality and meeting the learning targets are required to earn the full points needed to complete the mission. At the start of the quest, I make a map and guide of all the missions available as a HyperDoc on Google Classroom. **FIGURE 5.13** details two example missions with the tasks, expectations, and required evidence of learning, or you can scan the QR code to see the Dystopian Reading Quest in its entirety. For English language learners and students needing modifications, I provide a modified version of the quest that lists the required missions only, so as not to overwhelm them with the optional enrichment quests or a dauntingly long document.

**FULL
READING QUEST**

DYSTOPIAN READING QUEST (2017)

Complete the following badges throughout this unit to earn privileges and unlock powers (up to 2,000 XP). The more badges you complete toward mastery, and complete correctly, the more privileges you will gain as you unlock the Oracle of Dystopian Knowledge.

BADGE	TASKS	LEARNING TARGET	LINK/EVIDENCE
Apocalypse **100 XP**	*Read through the first three chapters of your dystopian text and complete the Google form. Support answers with textual evidence.* **Warnings:** How did people hope to create a more perfect world? What is the intended utopia? What could go wrong to create a terrifying dystopian world? **Laws:** List the laws of this society. Which are the ones that may cause problems? **Visitors:** As a visitor of this society, what do you see? What's going on there to make it a terrifying place to live for a majority of people? **Government:** Describe the government, the police, or those in charge. Why is it a problem? **Oppression:** Who is the oppressor in this dystopian world? Who is oppressed, and how are they oppressed?	**CCSS.ELA-Literacy.RL.8.1** Cite the textual evidence that most strongly supports an analysis of what the text says explicitly as well as inferences drawn from the text.	Completed Google form providing textual evidence used for each element of the dystopian controls
Frames of Mind **200 XP**	*Character & Character Development* 1. Complete the *Who is the protagonist* questionnaire available in Google Classroom. 2. Choose three different passages throughout your book to "peel the layers" of the protagonist and highlight the theories (and analysis) about this protagonist. Scan copies of the three passages, annotate, and show your thinking about the character in a one-page (at least) reflection and analysis about the protagonist's depth.	**CCSS.ELA-Literacy.RL.8.3** Analyze how particular lines of dialogue or incidents in a story propel the action, reveal aspects of character, or provoke a decision. **CCSS.ELA-Literacy.W.8.2** Write informative/explanatory texts to examine a topic and convey ideas, concepts, and information through the selection, organization, and analysis of relevant content.	1. Questionnaire 2. Close reading analysis written reflection

FIGURE 5.13 At the start of the Dystopian Reading Quest, students receive a mission guide (scan the QR code to see the full HyperDoc) so they can choose which missions to work on and in what order.

When students are working on quests, missions, and badges there is choice and work is self-paced. The variety of missions taps into multiple learning styles and levels. To succeed, students must be Creative Communicators throughout the missions, which require multiple technology mediums be used to express understanding in accordance with the ISTE Standards for Students (ISTE, 2016) and specific Common Core State Standards, as well.

CLASSCRAFT AND VISION QUESTS

In creating your own quest-based learning experience, think about what you want your students to be able to know, understand, and do. Depending on your students, it might be conducive to create a quest with specific missions that students have to complete at their own pace to meet grade-level learning targets. To create such a quest, you could dip into the world of Classcraft, a gaming platform that offers a quest interface with which you can build adventure-based learning experiences. The teacher, or gamemaster, can insert content-specific curriculum onto an interactive map for personalized learning. Because Classcraft is integrated with Google Classroom, assignments in Google Classroom can be imported into a quest for specifics tasks.

For example, for a social-justice reading unit, I used Classcraft to create a Social Justice Vision Quest (**FIGURE 5.14**). The first step to creating a quest on Classcraft is to set up an introduction and objective. Because each of the books students could read for the unit addressed a protagonist who stood up to injustice, I began the storyline for the quests with,

> *Throughout history there have been moments when people have been called upon to stand up for what is right. They have witnessed injustice, hatred, intolerance, and have decided that they cannot stand aside as a bystander. Who are these upstanders, and how do they change the course of history for all of humanity?*

FIGURE 5.14
On Classcraft.com, the Social Justice Vision Quest uses a map to highlight the various missions students must complete.

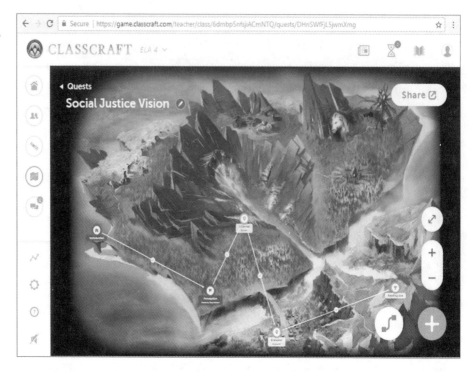

With the story established, I mapped out three sequential missions based on what the students should be able to know, do, and understand by the end of the unit. Students could complete the missions at their own pace, but had to finish them all in order.

The first mission, Perception, consisted of students answering basic comprehension questions about their reading of the first fifty pages of their text; they could choose to read *I Am Malala* (2013) by Malala Yousafzai, *Warriors Don't Cry* (2007) by Melba Pattillo Beals, or *All American Boys* (2015) by Jason Reynolds and Brendan Kiely. On a Google form, students answered specific questions related to their understanding of their book's characters, settings, events, vocabulary in context, and emerging themes. In order to unlock the second mission, Alliances, students needed to answer all of the questions correctly on the Google Quiz.

The beginning of the Alliance mission stated,

> *We often look to models and mentors for wisdom. These people's lives are a testament that being an upstander takes strength and perseverance.*

For the Alliances mission, students read an article about Ghandi then completed a short response assignment that required them to identify a quote from Gandhi's teachings and show evidence of Gandhi's philosophy in their protagonist's actions. If the written response adequately met the learning target of making text-to-text connections, the third mission was unlocked. If a student did not meet the learning target, he or she was required to revise the short response until achieving the reading and writing standard.

The story behind the third mission, Evaluator, started,

> *When we get to the end of a story our minds are filled with questions, thoughts, connections, and reflections. Many of the elements presented in the book you read are grounded in history and current events. What elements of your dystopian text are more reality than fiction? What statement might the author be trying to make about our world today and humanity?*

Before you make it to the end of the Social Justice Vision Quest, you must complete the Evaluator Mission.

The task in this last mission was for students to showcase their understanding of their social justice book in a single-page assignment called a One-Pager. Either technology-based or created with traditional pencil and paper, a One-Pager is a creative way for students to show their unique understanding of the text. For the Social Justice Vision Quest, I asked students to include the title of their book, notable quotes that struck them, a visual image to illustrate the pictures they had in their minds from reading, short responses to specific questions, and

BUILD YOUR OWN QUEST

QUEST TEMPLATE

Whether you use a game-creation platform or plain pencil and paper, creating a plan or template makes designing quests and missions easier. For example, I often use the template in Grant Wiggins and Jay McTighe's *Understanding By Design* (2005) to help me design missions. To offer you the same sort of assistance, I designed the template shown in **FIGURE 5.15**. You can use it to plan the narrative, tasks, learning targets, and more. (To make as many copies as you need, scan the QR code.)

When planning a quest, where do you start? Based on the Understanding by Design® Framework, Stage 1 is identifying the desired results: what will students understand, know, and do? You can start at the bottom of the table and write the long-term end results first. Sometimes I am inspired by a game or a story that helps the activities unfold. Game themes or the storyline can be based on actual board games, video games, and game shows. The storyline of a game can also be based on the unit of study, a book, a movie, or a theme.

Even if you are not clear on the story and context of the adventure-based mission, once you have identified your learning goals, you can move on to Stage 2, the planning stage for the tasks. Wiggins and McTighe include this stage to "determine assessment evidence" and performance assessments. These tasks might require students to read, write, answer questions and apply their understanding, or demonstrate a new skill. The key is the alignment with the end results and all the tasks or missions.

Once you have articulated the tasks, Stage 3 has you plan learning experiences to support the diverse learners in your classroom. This stage helps create the differentiated paths for diverse learners. Lastly, it's time to clarify the storyline and context throughout the quest. The storyline drives the entire adventure-based experience, and you want to hook your student with meaningful and authentic tasks that meet your learning goals.

Adventure-Based Learning, Missions, & Quests

Topic/Title:

The Story (The introduction is a fictional (or not!) story to introduce students to the objective. Adding a narrative element is a good way to gamify your lesson: When students progress in the lesson, they're also progressing through the story):		
MISSION 1:		
Story/Contex	What is the story, context or theme of Mission 1? What key facts do students need? What details will immerse students in the mission story? What parts of the mission do you want to reveal in Mission 1?	
Task	What are your objectives? What will students accomplish? What learning targets do students have to meet to complete the mission?	
Differentiated Paths	Thinking of the diverse learners in your classroom: Is there a modified task that some students might take to get to the same outcomes? What different task will these students complete?	
Rewards	What will students earn or receive for completing the mission?	
MISSION 2:		
Story/Context	What key facts/story details will Mission 2 reveal?	
Task	What are your objectives? What will students accomplish? What learning targets do students have to meet to complete the mission?	
Differentiated Paths	Thinking of the diverse learners in your classroom: Is there a modified task that some students might take to get to the same outcomes? What different task will these students complete?	
Rewards	What will students earn or receive for completing the mission?	
MISSION 3:		
Story/Context	What key facts/story details will Mission 3 reveal?	
Task	What are your objectives? What will students accomplish? What learning targets do students have to meet to complete the mission?	
Differentiated Paths	Thinking of the diverse learners in your classroom: Is there a modified task that some students might take to get to the same outcomes? What different task will these students complete?	
Rewards	What will students earn or receive for completing the mission?	
END RESULT:		
Now that students have completed the final mission, what have they learned, gained, and earned? Is there a cliffhanger or the possibility of a second installment in the works? Are you leading students to a new adventure or has the game ended here?		

FIGURE 5.15 To build a quest adventure for your students, you need to brainstorm the missions and activities (games, academic pursuits, and physical tasks), as well as the narrative story they are centered around.

a personal statement about what they read (**FIGURE 5.16**). The One-Pager summative assessment, like the missions themselves, can be anything that enables students to show their thinking, understanding, and synthesis of their reading.

For more ideas and examples of gamifying your lessons, check out my previous book, *Gamify Literacy: Boost Comprehension, Collaboration and Learning* (2017), in which educators share lessons and experiences about using gamification in their classrooms.

FIGURE 5.16

The One-Pager assignment allows students to showcase thinking, connections, visualization, and response to text-based questions.

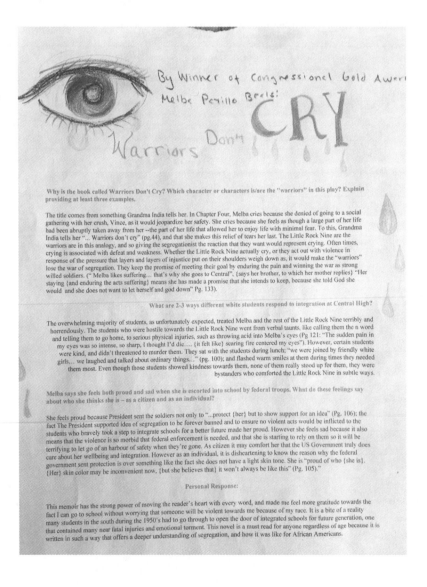

GLOBAL COLLABORATIVE PROJECTS: LEARN FROM EACH OTHER

Working with others is a key skill that students need to succeed in our digital and global world today. Collaboration is learned, and, as teachers, we cannot assume that all students know how to work well with one another to accomplish a goal. Collaborative activities in the classroom help to build community and practice communication skills. Beyond the walls of our classrooms, global collaboration is an innovative teaching tool that helps prepare students to become active participants in our global community, celebrates diverse cultures, and supports student learning. Global collaborative projects tap into many of the existing and emerging skills and literacies required of teachers and students: listening, reading, writing, speaking, problem solving, creating, and using technology to practice digital citizenship. In fact, collaboration is included throughout the Common Core State Standards and ISTE Standards for Students (see the Appendix for details).

You can participate in one of the many global collaborative projects that currently exist (**TABLE 5.1**), or you can create your own by making connections with other teachers around the globe through Twitter, ISTE professional learning networks (PLNs), or Edmodo. Global partnerships are about making connections with other teachers and schools to benefit all students' learning. A successful project is interactive and engaging, while also revolving around real questions and problems. For example, I developed a partnership with a school in Japan through the Japan Society, whose Going Global Social Networking Project matches teachers in the U.S. with teachers in Japan to expand their students' worldview of different cultures. The pairing was a good fit, because my school has a large Japanese community. The Japanese students in my class took center stage during the project, helping teach their classmates basic Japanese language and about the culture. This allowed all the students to learn more about Japanese culture and their ELL peers to be experts. My counterpart in Japan and I first established a pen pal exchange among the students to introduce each other, build community, and have a "handshake." We wrote via postal mail, but you could also correspond through email, discussion platforms like Edmodo, or a collaborative website like a wiki.

MODEL COLLABORATION AND COMMUNICATION

With any global collaborative project, prior to contacting your partner class, spend some time setting up the project with students, teaching netiquette, and discussing responsible digital citizenship. Not only will this ensure a better experience in the project, you'll be reinforcing ISTE Standards for Students 2a and 2b (ISTE, 2016). Likewise, while they're adapting to language barriers and cultural differences, be ready to support students and facilitate successful collaboration and communication. Students need to know what respectful and considerate cooperative work looks like and sounds like. Model positive communication for successful collaboration, offer guidelines, and even provide specific communication starters for students. In Stephanie Harvey and Harvey Daniels' *Comprehension and Collaboration: Inquiry Circles in Action* (2009), you can find a thorough list of communication starters to help students articulate respect and tolerance including, "I am glad that you brought that up," "I would have never thought of that," and "I agree with what you are saying" (p. 47).

To help initiate a discussion about working with others, for instance, offer students different scenarios of typical collaboration challenges they may encounter and ask them to brainstorm positive responses. Here are some I gave my students to consider:

+ One student in a small group acts as a dictator and completes all the work. Other group members take a backseat in the project, because the one person has taken over everyone's jobs. What should the group do without hurting anyone's feelings?

+ Miscommunication among the group members results in some people working on the wrong assignment while others are completely confused. How can this group get back on track to finish the assignment accurately?

✦ One group member's contributions are inaccurate. The other group members do not want to hurt the student's feelings, but the work is wrong. What should this group do?

Effective communication hinges on the practice and modeling of positive cooperation and collaboration. When participating in a global collaborative project, remind students to keep language clear and specific, so they can be more effective communicators and meet project objectives.

RYE, NEW YORK, AND KYOTO, JAPAN'S GLOBAL CONNECTIONS

Creating a successful global collaborative project requires much planning. Whether participating in an already existing global project or creating your own, be sure clear goals and outcomes are communicated with all participants. Global collaboration projects can follow any path that benefits the classrooms involved, or, as in my case, a curriculum organized by the facilitating organization. Working with a class from the Kyoto International School through the Going Global Social Networking Project, students completed three elements.

First, my students in Rye, New York, and their counterparts in Kyoto, Japan, participated in an introductory assignment where, individually or with a partner in their class, they created written blog posts or digital videos about themselves and their community. Students shared these videos and blog posts online using the Japan Society's secure social networking site, Going Global. This introductory blog allowed students to introduce themselves to the global participants and share information about their own cultural interests. Students had the option of taking pictures of their community to include in their posts for a visual perspective. Students are interested in what schools and neighborhoods look like in another country. When students share these visual elements, they are able to see the commonalities and differences among all the participants, but such sharing also initiates inquiry and interest among students. Global collaboration works well when there are introduction prompts for students to share and make connections across the globe with other young people. At the same time, global collaboration requires open communication and planning with all teachers involved.

After the initial pen pal letters and handshake, students viewed two Disney animated films—*Tangled* (2010) and *Brave* (2012)—with their own classes, followed by two Japanese animes by Hayao Miyazaki—*My Neighbor Totoro* (English language dub, 2005) and *Spirited Away* (2001). After their viewings, the two classes then came together to discuss the movies by sharing posts on the Going Global platform. For our project, students shared written responses, but your students also could use FaceTime, Skype, or Google Hangouts for discussions if time zones allow.

In both our classes and online, viewing these movies led to a discussion about the roles of gender, age, race, and ethnicity, as they were presented in the animated films and in our respective cultures. After viewing and discussing the films in our respective classes and online, students worked in small groups that consisted of classmates and global students, to research and write a collaborative report on an assigned critical theory regarding race and ethnicity, gender, or age. Using Wikispaces, a social writing platform for educators to make classroom webpages, the groups posted their reports to the class wiki. Working in a collaborative web platform, such as a wiki or Edmodo, students can collaborate and post work at any time. Because my students and their Kyoto partners were working in different time zones and not necessarily working daily on the project, students frequently had to wait for feedback from their Japanese counterparts. Handwritten responses via postal mail took even longer, but students were most excited to receive these, because they were more personal.

Due to the diverse nature of students in each of the classes, each component of the project was scaffolded for the diverse range of student abilities. Students received models, checklists, and assessment rubrics so they knew the project's expectations. The teacher in Japan and I were in constant email conversation to help the project run smoothly and support our students.

TABLE 5.1   FIVE GLOBAL COLLABORATIVE PROJECTS TO GET INVOLVED

Created to promote the love of reading and connect readers around the world, The Global Read Aloud is a six-week event starting in October. Participating teachers and students commit to reading aloud the year's selected book and to connecting with as many other participating classes around the globe as possible. Classes connect and share reading responses through Skype, Twitter, Edmodo, or Write About as determined by the teachers. Each year a range of titles—from picture books to young adult books—is selected, so all grades can participate.

With Mystery Skypes, classrooms video chat with each other via Skype and try to guess where in the world the other classroom is located. Microsoft in Education has an entire webpage to help teachers get started.

iEARN is an organization that supports more than 150 global projects designed and facilitated by teachers and students. Every project proposed must answer the question, "How will this project improve the quality of life on the planet?" The focus is on global collaboration and global citizenship. iEARN can help you if you are looking for a partner for your global project idea or looking to join a global project.

The Center for Innovation in Engineering and Science Education at Stevens Institute of Technology focuses on science and offers fourteen collaborative projects, covering a variety of projects from temperature to human genetics to water purification. Projects are available for students in grades 1–12.

Flat Connections coordinates major international collaboration projects including Global Youth Debates, Digiteen, Windows to the World, and more. For step-by-step details about the Flat Connections collaborations and setting up global collaboration projects, a good resource is *Flattening Classrooms, Engaging Minds* (2013) by Julie Lindsay and Vicki Davis.

AS YOU GO FORWARD: WHY PERSONALIZED LEARNING AND DIGITAL LITERACY MATTER

Despite all the digital demands on our students' attention, we teachers are not competing with technology. Rather, technology allows us (and our students) to curate personalized learning and reading experiences that expand student knowledge and promote critical thinking, digital citizenship, and the literacy skills of proficient readers. When used thoughtfully and purposefully, technology tools can help our students understand their world and ignite a passion in learning. For students to see the purpose and the promise that school can offer, we educators need to think creatively about how students get information and how they can demonstrate their learning.

Learning today is blended, personalized, and digital. Teachers are facilitators, coaching students through deep learning. As Fisher, Frey, and Hattie stated in *Visible Learning for Literacy* (2016), our purpose as teachers is "engaging students in the best learning opportunities" (p. xiii) we can for the transfer of knowledge. How do we engage and motivate our students to read and to learn? When we create lessons with purpose and our students' individual needs in mind, all students can achieve more. Providing choice, blending learning opportunities, and incorporating technology lifts the level of engagement and understanding.

The ideas presented throughout this book are not magical one-size-fits-all lessons for everyone. They are examples to remind us as teachers to engage *all* students with creative and innovative activities. In doing so, we are able to help students not only to meet the standards, but, more importantly, to build the independence and critical thinking to read words and the world. We want students to grapple with information and tackle tough texts while utilizing technology supports and reading strategies to help comprehend and think critically about the text. We want reluctant readers to find a text that captures their attention and pulls them in to want to read and learn more. We want our English language learners to be part of classroom discussions and activities so they can actively participate and contribute. We want to challenge our advanced readers in relevant and meaningful ways. We want our students to work together collaboratively and understand that we all have something worthwhile to bring to the table. To do all of this, we need to know our students and personalize reading to empower our students as learners so that they can go on to succeed in school and beyond.

TABLE 5.2   PAIRING TOOLS WITH TEACHING STRATEGIES

TEACHING STRATEGY (PEDAGOGY)	TECHNOLOGY TOOL	LINK
Flipped Lessons	Screencast-O-Matic	screencast-o-matic.com
	YouTube	youtube.com
Choice menus	Adobe Voice	spark.adobe.com
	Animoto	animoto.com
	Audacity	audacityteam.org
	#BookSnaps	taramartin.com
	Educreations	educreations.com
	Glogster	edu.glogster.com
	Google Suite	edu.google.com
	Haiku Deck	haikudeck.com
	iMovie	apple.com/imovie
	Kahoot!	kahoot.com
	LiveBinders	livebinders.com
	PowToon	powtoon.com
	Prezi	prezi.com
	TED Talks	ted.org
	Tellagami	tellagami.com
	ThingLink	thinglink.com
	Toondoo	toondoo.com

COMMON CORE STATE STANDARDS	ISTE STANDARDS FOR STUDENTS AND FOR EDUCATORS
CCSS.ELA-Literacy.CCRA.R.1 Read closely to determine what the text says explicitly and to make logical inferences from it; cite specific textual evidence when writing or speaking to support conclusions drawn from the text.	(E) 3b. Citizen Establish a learning culture that promotes curiosity and critical examination of online resources and fosters digital literacy and media fluency.
CCSS.ELA-Literacy.CCRA.SL.5 Make strategic use of digital media and visual displays of data to express information and enhance understanding of presentations.	(S) 3. Knowledge Constructor Students critically curate a variety of resources using digital tools to construct knowledge, produce creative artifacts, and make meaningful learning experiences for themselves and others.

continues on next page

TABLE 5.2   PAIRING TOOLS WITH TEACHING STRATEGIES, *CONTINUED*

TEACHING STRATEGY (PEDAGOGY)	TECHNOLOGY TOOL	LINK
Genius Hour and Passion Projects	Audacity	audacityteam.org
	Blogger	blogger.com
	Breakout EDU	breakoutedu.com
	Digital Inspirations	beyondliteracylink.blogspot.com
	GoAnimate	goanimate.com
	Screencasting	screencast-o-matic.com
	Snapguides	snapguide.com
	TED Talks	ted.org
Gamification and quest-based learning	Classcraft	classcraft.com
Global collaborative projects	Edmodo	edmodo.com
	Flat Connections	flatconnections.com
	The Global Read Aloud	theglobalreadaloud.com
	iEARN	iearn.org
	Japan Society	japansociety.org
	Mystery Skypes	education.microsoft.com
	Skype	skype.com
	Wikispaces	wikispaces.com
	Write About	writeabout.com
	Center for Engineering and Science Education at Stevens Institute of Technology	k12science.org

COMMON CORE STATE STANDARDS	ISTE STANDARDS FOR STUDENTS AND FOR EDUCATORS
CSS.ELA-Literacy.CCRA.SL.5 Make strategic use of digital media and visual displays of data to express information and enhance understanding of presentations.	(E) 5. Designer Educators design authentic, learner-driven activities and environments that recognize and accommodate learner variability.
CCSS.ELA-Literacy.CCRA.R.2 Determine central ideas or themes of a text and analyze their development; summarize the key supporting details and ideas.	(S) 3c. Knowledge Constructor Students curate information from digital resources using a variety of tools and methods to create collections of artifacts that demonstrate meaningful connections or conclusions.
CCSS.ELA-Literacy.CCRA.SL.5 Make strategic use of digital media and visual displays of data to express information and enhance understanding of presentations. College and Career Readiness Anchor Standards: Speaking and Listening Prepare for and participate effectively in a range of conversations and collaborations with diverse partners, building on others' ideas and expressing their own clearly and persuasively.	(S) 7. Digital Citizen Students use digital tools to broaden their perspectives and enrich their learning by collaborating with others and working effectively in teams locally and globally.

ISTE STANDARDS

ISTE STANDARDS FOR STUDENTS

The ISTE Standards for Students emphasize the skills and qualities we want for students, enabling them to engage and thrive in a connected, digital world. The standards are designed for use by educators across the curriculum, with every age student, with a goal of cultivating these skills throughout a student's academic career. Both students and teachers will be responsible for achieving foundational technology skills to fully apply the standards. The reward, however, will be educators who skillfully mentor and inspire students to amplify learning with technology and challenge them to be agents of their own learning.

1. Empowered Learner

   Students leverage technology to take an active role in choosing, achieving and demonstrating competency in their learning goals, informed by the learning sciences. Students:

   a. articulate and set personal learning goals, develop strategies leveraging technology to achieve them and reflect on the learning process itself to improve learning outcomes.

   b. build networks and customize their learning environments in ways that support the learning process.

   c. use technology to seek feedback that informs and improves their practice and to demonstrate their learning in a variety of ways.

   d. understand the fundamental concepts of technology operations, demonstrate the ability to choose, use and troubleshoot current technologies and are able to transfer their knowledge to explore emerging technologies.

2. Digital Citizen

Students recognize the rights, responsibilities and opportunities of living, learning and working in an interconnected digital world, and they act and model in ways that are safe, legal and ethical. Students:

a. cultivate and manage their digital identity and reputation and are aware of the permanence of their actions in the digital world.

b. engage in positive, safe, legal and ethical behavior when using technology, including social interactions online or when using networked devices.

c. demonstrate an understanding of and respect for the rights and obligations of using and sharing intellectual property.

d. manage their personal data to maintain digital privacy and security and are aware of data-collection technology used to track their navigation online.

3. Knowledge Constructor

Students critically curate a variety of resources using digital tools to construct knowledge, produce creative artifacts and make meaningful learning experiences for themselves and others. Students:

a. plan and employ effective research strategies to locate information and other resources for their intellectual or creative pursuits.

b. evaluate the accuracy, perspective, credibility and relevance of information, media, data or other resources.

c. curate information from digital resources using a variety of tools and methods to create collections of artifacts that demonstrate meaningful connections or conclusions.

d. build knowledge by actively exploring real-world issues and problems, developing ideas and theories and pursuing answers and solutions.

4. Innovative Designer

   Students use a variety of technologies within a design process to identify and solve problems by creating new, useful or imaginative solutions. Students:

   a. know and use a deliberate design process for generating ideas, testing theories, creating innovative artifacts or solving authentic problems.

   b. select and use digital tools to plan and manage a design process that considers design constraints and calculated risks.

   c. develop, test and refine prototypes as part of a cyclical design process.

   d. exhibit a tolerance for ambiguity, perseverance and the capacity to work with open-ended problems.

5. Computational Thinker

   Students develop and employ strategies for understanding and solving problems in ways that leverage the power of technological methods to develop and test solutions. Students:

   a. formulate problem definitions suited for technology-assisted methods such as data analysis, abstract models and algorithmic thinking in exploring and finding solutions.

   b. collect data or identify relevant data sets, use digital tools to analyze them, and represent data in various ways to facilitate problem-solving and decision-making.

   c. break problems into component parts, extract key information, and develop descriptive models to understand complex systems or facilitate problem-solving.

   d. understand how automation works and use algorithmic thinking to develop a sequence of steps to create and test automated solutions.

6. Creative Communicator

Students communicate clearly and express themselves creatively for a variety of purposes using the platforms, tools, styles, formats and digital media appropriate to their goals. Students:

   a. choose the appropriate platforms and tools for meeting the desired objectives of their creation or communication.

   b. create original works or responsibly repurpose or remix digital resources into new creations.

   c. communicate complex ideas clearly and effectively by creating or using a variety of digital objects such as visualizations, models or simulations.

   d. publish or present content that customizes the message and medium for their intended audiences.

7. Global Collaborator

Students use digital tools to broaden their perspectives and enrich their learning by collaborating with others and working effectively in teams locally and globally. Students:

   a. use digital tools to connect with learners from a variety of backgrounds and cultures, engaging with them in ways that broaden mutual understanding and learning.

   b. use collaborative technologies to work with others, including peers, experts or community members, to examine issues and problems from multiple viewpoints.

   c. contribute constructively to project teams, assuming various roles and responsibilities to work effectively toward a common goal.

   d. explore local and global issues and use collaborative technologies to work with others to investigate solutions.

ISTE STANDARDS FOR EDUCATORS

The ISTE Standards for Educators are your road map to helping students become empowered learners. These standards will deepen your practice, promote collaboration with peers, challenge you to rethink traditional approaches and prepare students to drive their own learning.

EMPOWERED PROFESSIONAL

1. Learner

Educators continually improve their practice by learning from and with others and exploring proven and promising practices that leverage technology to improve student learning. Educators:

a. Set professional learning goals to explore and apply pedagogical approaches made possible by technology and reflect on their effectiveness.

b. Pursue professional interests by creating and actively participating in local and global learning networks.

c. Stay current with research that supports improved student learning outcomes, including findings from the learning sciences.

2. Leader

Educators seek out opportunities for leadership to support student empowerment and success and to improve teaching and learning. Educators:

a. Shape, advance and accelerate a shared vision for empowered learning with technology by engaging with education stakeholders.

b. Advocate for equitable access to educational technology, digital content and learning opportunities to meet the diverse needs of all students.

c. Model for colleagues the identification, exploration, evaluation, curation and adoption of new digital resources and tools for learning.

3. Citizen

   Educators inspire students to positively contribute to and responsibly participate in the digital world. Educators:

   a. Create experiences for learners to make positive, socially responsible contributions and exhibit empathetic behavior online that build relationships and community.

   b. Establish a learning culture that promotes curiosity and critical examination of online resources and fosters digital literacy and media fluency.

   c. Mentor students in safe, legal and ethical practices with digital tools and the protection of intellectual rights and property.

   d. Model and promote management of personal data and digital identity and protect student data privacy.

LEARNING CATALYST

1. Collaborator

   Educators dedicate time to collaborate with both colleagues and students to improve practice, discover and share resources and ideas, and solve problems. Educators:

   a. Dedicate planning time to collaborate with colleagues to create authentic learning experiences that leverage technology.

   b. Collaborate and colearn with students to discover and use new digital resources and diagnose and troubleshoot technology issues.

   c. Use collaborative tools to expand students' authentic, real-world learning experiences by engaging virtually with experts, teams and students, locally and globally.

   d. Demonstrate cultural competency when communicating with students, parents and colleagues and interact with them as cocollaborators in student learning.

2. Designer

   Educators design authentic, learner-driven activities and environments that recognize and accommodate learner variability. Educators:

   a. Use technology to create, adapt and personalize learning experiences that foster independent learning and accommodate learner differences and needs.

   b. Design authentic learning activities that align with content area standards and use digital tools and resources to maximize active, deep learning.

   c. Explore and apply instructional design principles to create innovative digital learning environments that engage and support learning.

3. Facilitator

   Educators facilitate learning with technology to support student achievement of the 2016 ISTE Standards for Students. Educators:

   a. Foster a culture where students take ownership of their learning goals and outcomes in both independent and group settings.

   b. Manage the use of technology and student learning strategies in digital platforms, virtual environments, hands-on makerspaces or in the field.

   c. Create learning opportunities that challenge students to use a design process and computational thinking to innovate and solve problems.

   d. Model and nurture creativity and creative expression to communicate ideas, knowledge or connections.

4. Analyst

Educators understand and use data to drive their instruction and support students in achieving their learning goals. Educators:

a. Provide alternative ways for students to demonstrate competency and reflect on their learning using technology.

b. Use technology to design and implement a variety of formative and summative assessments that accommodate learner needs, provide timely feedback to students and inform instruction.

c. Use assessment data to guide progress and communicate with students, parents and education stakeholders to build student self-direction.

© 2017 International Society for Technology in Education.

REFERENCES

Abbott, E. A. (1884). *Flatland: A romance of many dimensions*. London, UK: Seeley & Co.

Alban, T., Guthrie, J. T., Schafer, C. & Von Secker, C. (2000). Contributions of instructional practices to reading achievement in a statewide improvement program. *The Journal of Educational Research, 93*(4), 211–225.

Allington, R. (2013). *What really matters for middle school readers: From research to practice*. What really matters series. Hoboken, NJ: Pearson Education.

Anderson, H. L., Fisher, D., Frey, N. & Thayre, M. (2015). *Text dependent questions, grades 6-12: Pathways to close and critical reading*. Thousand Oaks, CA: Corwin Literacy.

Applegate, K. A. (2012). *The one and only Ivan*. New York, NY: HarperCollins.

Arnold, D. (2016). *Kids of appetite*. New York, NY: Viking Books for Young Readers.

Arora, G., Pousman, B., Kakoulides, S., Storr, S., Fabien, C., & Keating, K. (Producers), & Arora, G. & Pousman, B. (Directors). (2015). *Clouds over Sidra: A virtual reality experience* [Short film]. United States: Here Be Dragons.

Aveyard, V. (2015). *Red queen*. Vol 1. Red queen series. New York, NY: HarperCollins.

Aveyard, V. (2016). *Glass sword*. Vol 2. Red queen series. New York, NY: HarperCollins.

Beah, I. (2007). *A long way gone: Memoirs of a boy soldier*. New York, NY: Sarah Crichton Books/Farrar, Straus and Giroux.

Beals, M. P. (2007). *Warriors don't cry: A searing memoir of the battle to integrate Little Rock's Central High*. New York, NY: Simon Pulse.

Beers, K. & Probst, R. E. (2017). *Disrupting thinking: Why how we read matters*. New York, NY: Scholastic Teaching Resources.

Calkins, L. M. (2000). *The art teaching reading*. Hoboken, NJ: Pearson Education.

Carreker, S. (2017, December 12). *Strategies to support non-proficient adolescent readers: Identifying and addressing why they struggle* [White paper]. Retrieved from lexialearning.com/resources/white-papers/supporting-non-proficient-adolescent-readers

Chernin, P., Gigliotti, D., Melfi, T., Topping, J., & Williams, P. (Producers), & Melfi, T. (Director). (2016). *Hidden figures* [Motion picture]. United States: Twentieth Century Fox Film Corporation.

Conli, R. (Producer), Greno, N. & Howard, B. (Directors). (2010). *Tangled* [Motion picture]. United States: Walt Disney Pictures.

Conniff, R. (2012, June). When continental drift was considered pseudoscience. *Smithsonian Magazine*. Retrieved from smithsonianmag.com/science-nature/when-continental-drift-was-considered-pseudoscience-90353214

D'Alessandro, A. (2014, April 7). 22 facts about plastic pollution (and 10 things we can do about it). *EcoWatch*. Retrieved from ecowatch.com/22-facts-about-plastic-pollution-and-10-things-we-can-do-about-it-1881885971.html

Daniels, H. & Steineke, N. (2011). *Texts and lessons for content-area reading: With more than 75 articles from The New York Times, Rolling Stone, The Washington Post, Car and Driver, Chicago Tribune, and many others*. Portsmouth, NH: Heinemann.

Dede, C. (2016, November 7). *Preparing students for the future workforce*. [Lecture]. Superintendent's Conference Day, Rye City School District, Rye, NY.

Ernst, D., Lasseter, J., & Suzuki, T. (Producers), & Miyazaki, H. (Director). (2001). *Spirited away* [Motion picture]. United States: Walt Disney Pictures.

Extence, G. (2013). *The universe versus Alex Woods*. London, UK: Hodder & Stoughton Ltd.

Ferriss, T. (Producer), & Ferriss, T. & Isaacson, W. (Presenters). (2017, October 14). Lessons from Steve Jobs, Leonardo da Vinci, and Ben Franklin. *The Tim Ferriss Show*. Podcast retrieved from tim.blog/2017/10/14/walter-isaacson

Fisher, D. & Frey, N. (2014). *Close reading and writing from sources*. Newark, DE: International Reading Association.

Fisher, D., Frey, N., & Hattie, J. (2016). *Visible learning for literacy: Implementing the practices that work best to accelerate student learning grades k-12.* Thousand Oaks, CA: Corwin Literacy.

Fleming, C. (2014). *The family Romanov: Murder, rebellion, and the fall of imperial Russia*. New York, NY: Schwartz & Wade Books.

Freeman, Y. S. & Freeman, D. E. (2008). *Academic language for English language learners and struggling readers: How to help students succeed across content areas*. Portsmouth, NH: Heinemann.

Frey, J. (Director). (2014). *The present* [Animated short]. Germany: Filmakademie Baden-Wuerttemberg. Retrieved from vimeo.com/152985022

Furman, L. R. (2015). *Technology, reading & digital literacy: Strategies to engage the reluctant reader*. Eugene, OR: International Society for Technology in Education.

Gallagher, K. (2003). *Deeper reading: Comprehending challenging texts, 4–12.* Portland, ME: Stenhouse Publishers.

Gallagher, K. (2009). *Readicide: How schools are killing reading and what you can do about it.* Portland, ME: Stenhouse Publishers.

Gallagher, K. (2015). *In the best interest of students: Staying true to what works in the ELA classroom*. Portland, ME: Stenhouse Publishers.

Gladwell, M. (2008). *Outliers: The story of success*. New York : Little, Brown and Co.

Godin, S. (2010). *Linchpin: Are you indispensable?* New York, NY: Penguin Group.

Goldberg, G. (2015). *Mindsets and Moves: Strategies that help readers take charge [grades K–8]*. Thousand Oaks, CA: Corwin.

Gonzalez, J. (2016, September 4). Using playlists to differentiate instruction [Blog post]. Retrieved from cultofpedagogy.com/student-playlists-differentiation

Gonzalez, J. (2017, June 11). How HyperDocs can transform your teaching [Blog post]. Retrieved from cultofpedagogy.com/hyperdocs

Google. (2018). *Google Expeditions* [Website]. Retrieved from edu.google.com/expeditions/#about

Green, J. (2012). *The fault in our stars*. New York, NY: Dutton Books.

Greenberg, M. (Producer), & Unseld, S. (Director). (2013). *The blue umbrella* [Animated short]. United States: Pixar Animation Studios. Retrieved from vimeo.com/220616089

Haiken, M. (2017). *Gamify literacy: Boost comprehension, collaboration and learning*. Eugene, OR: International Society for Technology in Education.

Hara, T. & Lott, N. (Producers), & Miyazaki, H. (Director). (2005). *My neighbor Totoro* [Motion Picture]. United States: Walt Disney Studios Home Entertainment.

Harvey, S. & Daniels, H. (2009). *Comprehension & collaboration: Inquiry circles in action*. Portsmouth, NH: Heinemann.

Harvey, S. & Goudvis, A. (2007). *Strategies that work: Teaching comprehension for understanding and engagement (2nd ed.)*. Portland, ME: Stenhouse Publishers.

Heil, J. (2017, October 14). *Technology, high expectations, and the art of relationships*. [Presentation]. EdTechTeam Google Summit, Manchester, CT.

Hesse, M. (2016). *Girl in the blue coat*. New York, NY: Little, Brown Books for Young Readers.

Highfill, L., Hilton, K. & Landis, S. (2016). *The HyperDoc handbook: Digital lesson design using Google apps*. Irvine, CA: EdTechTeam Press.

Hokes, C. (Producer), & Blaas, R. (Director). (2009). *Alma* [Animated short]. Spain: User T-38. Retrieved from youtube.com/watch?v=KPERcsZBqVY

Hunt, L. M. (2015). *Fish in a tree*. New York, NY: Nancy Paulsen Books.

International Society for Technology in Education. (2016). ISTE Standards for Students. Eugene, OR: International Society for Technology in Education. Retrieved from iste.org/standards/for-students

International Society for Technology in Education. (2017). ISTE Standards for Educators. Eugene, OR: International Society for Technology in Education. Retrieved from iste.org/standards/for-educators

Johansen, D. & Cherry-Paul, S. (2016). *Flip your writing workshop: A blended learning approach (1st ed.)*. Portsmouth, NH: Heinemann.

Jonker, T. & Sharp, C. (Producers), & Thomas, A. (Presenter). (2017, October 21). #56 Angie Thomas—The hate u give unraveled. *The Yarn*. Retrieved from player.fm/series/the-yarn/56-angie-thomas-the-hate-u-give-unraveled

Kittle, P. (2012). *Book love: Developing depth, stamina, and passion in adolescent readers (1st ed.)*. Portsmouth, NH: Heinemann.

Knowles, J. (1959). *A separate peace*. New York, NY: Secker & Warburg.

Lacombe, R. (Director). (2010). *Kwa Heri mandima* [Short film]. Switzerland: École Cantonale d'Art de Lausanne. Retrieved from youtube.com/watch?v=hef6Roa2z3U&t=56s

Lan, X. (Producer & Director). (2016). *You look scary* [Animated short]. United States: CalArts. Retrieved from vimeo.com/163109106

Layne, S. (2015). *In defense of read-aloud: Sustaining best practice*. Portland, ME: Stenhouse Publishers.

Lee, H. (1960). *To kill a mockingbird*. Philadelphia, PA: Lippincott.

Lichtman, F. & Shattuck, S. (Producers & Directors). (2015). *Animated life: Pangea, Wegener, and continental drift* [Animated short]. United States: Howard Hughes Medical Institute. Retrieved from hhmi.org/biointeractive/animated-life-pangea

Lindsay, J. & Davis, V. (2013). *Flattening classrooms, engaging minds: Move to global collaboration one step at a time*. Pearson resources for 21st century learning. Hoboken, NJ: Pearson Education.

Lowry, L. (1993). *The giver*. New York, NY: Houghton Mifflin Books for Children.

Maiers, A. (2017). *Genius matters: A framework for epic transformation*. Lynbrook, NY: Choose2Matter, Inc.

Maiers, A. & Moran, M. (2016). *Liberating genius: A framework for epic transformation*. Lynbrook, NY: Choose2Matter, Inc.

Maiers, A. & Sandoval, A. (2011). *The passion-driven classroom: a framework for teaching and learning*. New York, NY: Routledge.

Martin, T. M. (2016, August 23). #BookSnaps—Snapping for learning [Blog post]. Retrieved from tarammartin.com/booksnaps-snapping-for-learning

McGregor, K. & Treuting, J. (Producers & Directors). (2015). *Mo's Bows* [Short film]. United States: Squirrel Friends. Retrieved from vimeo.com/120253654

Melvin, L. (2017). *Chasing space: Young readers' edition*. New York, NY: Amistad.

Miller, D. (2009). *The book whisperer: Awakening the inner reader in every child (1st ed.)*. San Francisco, CA: Jossey-Bass.

Miller, D. (2013). *Reading in the wild: The book whisperer's keys to cultivating lifelong reading habits (1st ed.)*. San Francisco, CA: Jossey-Bass.

Muhtaris, K. & Ziemke, K. (2015). *Amplify: Digital teaching and learning in the K-6 classroom*. Portsmouth, NH: Heinemann.

National Governors Association Center for Best Practices, & Council of Chief State School Officers. (2010). Common Core State Standards for English Language Arts. Retrieved from corestandards.org/ELA-Literacy

Orwell, G. (1990). *Animal farm*. New York, NY: Houghton Mifflin Books.

Pakula, A. (Producer), & Mulligan, R. (Director). (1962). *To kill a mockingbird* [Motion picture]. United States: Universal International Pictures.

Palacio, R. J. (2012). *Wonder*. New York, NY: Knopf.

Parris, H., Estrada, L. M., & Honigsfeld, A. M. (2017). *ELL frontiers: Using technology to enhance instruction for English learners (1st ed.)*. Thousand Oaks, CA: Corwin.

Pearson, P. D., Duffy, G. G., Roehler L. R. & Dole, J. (1991). Moving from the old to the new: Research on reading comprehension instruction. *Review of Educational Research, 61*(2), 239–264.

Pink, D. H. (2011). *Drive: The surprising truth about what motivates us*. New York, NY: Riverhead Books.

Pink, D. (2011). The genius hour: How 60 minutes a week can electrify your job [Blog post]. Retrieved from danpink.com/2011/07/the-genius-hour-how-60-minutes-a-week-can-electrify-your-job

Pollan, M. (2015). *The omnivore's dilemma: The secrets behind what you eat, young readers edition*. New York, NY: Dial Books.

Reynolds, J. & Kiely, B. (2015). *All American boys*. New York, NY: Antheneum Books for Young Readers.

Robb, L. (2010). *Teaching reading in middle school: A strategic approach to teaching reading that improves comprehension and thinking (2nd ed.)*. New York, NY: Scholastic Teaching Resources.

Salinger, J. D. (1951). *The catcher in the rye*. Boston, MA: Little, Brown and Company.

Sarafian, K. (Producer), & Andrews, M., Chapman, B., & Purcell, S. (Directors). (2012). *Brave* [Motion picture]. United States: Pixar Animation Studios, Walt Disney Pictures.

Scieszka, J. (2016). *Walt Disney's Alice in wonderland (2nd ed.)*. White Plains, NY: Disney Press.

Shusterman, N. (2009). *Unwind*. Vol. 1. Unwind dystology. New York, NY: Simon & Schuster Books for Young Readers.

Sondheimer, M. (Producer), & Barillaro, A. (Director). (2016). *Piper*. [Animated short]. United States: Pixar Animation Studios.

Spielberg, A. & Bahrani, R. (Producers), & Bahrani, R. (Director). (2009). *Plastic bag* [Short film]. United States: Noruz Films, Inc. Retrieved from vimeo.com/144928861

@SteeleThoughts. (2018, January 16). "It is good to know content. It is great to know pedagogy. It's imperative to know the kids" [Tweet]. Retrieved from twitter.com/SteeleThoughts/status/953315645113937920

Sturtevant, J. A. (2017). *Hacking engagement again: 50 teacher tools that will make students love your class*: Vol 12. Hack learning series. Cleveland, OH: Times 10 Publications.

Sulla, N. (2011). *Students taking charge: Inside the learner-active technology-infused classroom*. New York, NY: Routledge.

Tankersley, K. (2005). *Literacy strategies for grades 4–12: Reinforcing the threads of reading*. Alexandria, VA: Association for Supervision and Curriculum Development.

TeachThought. (2013). *The definition of the flipped classroom* [Blog post]. Retrieved from teachthought.com/learning/the-definition-of-the-flipped-classroom

TEDxNextGenerationAsheville (2010, August 28). Birke Baehr: *What's wrong with our food system*. [Video]. Retrieved from ted.com/talks/birke_baehr_what_s_wrong_with_our_food_system

Thomas, A. (2017). *The Hate U Give*. New York, NY: HarperCollins Balzer + Bray.

Tomlinson, C. A. (2017). *How to differentiate instruction in academically diverse classrooms (3rd ed.)*. Alexandria, VA: Association for Supervision and Curriculum Development.

Tovani, C. (2000). *I read it, but I don't get it: Comprehension strategies for adolescent readers*. Portland, ME: Stenhouse Publishers.

Tovani, C. (2004). *Do I really have to teach reading? Content comprehension, grades 6-12*. Portland, ME: Stenhouse Publishers.

Voigt, C. (1982). *Dicey's song*: Vol. 2. The Tillerman Cycle. New York, NY: Atheneum Books for Young Readers.

Wiesel, E. (2006). *Night*. New York, NY: Hill and Wang.

Wiggins, G. & McTighe, J. (2005). *Understanding by design (2nd ed.)*. Alexandria, VA: Association for Supervision and Curriculum Development.

Wilson, C. & Schlossar, E. (2007). *Chew on this: Everything you don't want to know about fast food*. New York, NY: Houghton Mifflin Company.

Wolk, L. (2016). *Wolf hollow*. New York, NY: Dutton Children's Books.

Wolk, S. (2010). What should students read? *Phi Delta Kappa International, 91*(7), 8–16.

Yousafzai, M. (2016). *I am Malala: How one girl stood up for education and changed the world, young readers edition*. New York, NY: Little, Brown Books for Young Readers.

Ziemke, K. (2016, January/February). Balancing text and tech: How it isn't an either/or scenario. *Literacy Today,* 32–33. Retrieved from kristinziemke.com/blog/2017/4/23/balancing-text-and-tech-how-it-isnt-an-eitheror-scenario

INDEX

YOUR OPINION MATTERS:
TELL US HOW WE'RE DOING!

Your feedback helps ISTE create the best possible resources for teaching and learning in the digital age. Share your thoughts with the community or tell us how we're doing!

YOU CAN:

✦ Write a review at amazon.com or barnesandnoble.com.

✦ Mention this book on social media and follow ISTE on Twitter @iste, Facebook @ISTEconnects or Instagram @isteconnects.

✦ Email us at books@iste.org with your questions or comments.